SILVER·BURDETT

Making Music

Resource Book

Teacher's Edition Part Three
Grade 4

PEARSON

Scott
Foresman

Editorial Offices: Glenview, Illinois • Parsippany, New Jersey • New York, New York
Sales Offices: Needham, Massachusetts • Duluth, Georgia • Glenview, Illinois
Coppell, Texas • Sacramento, California • Mesa, Arizona

ISBN: 0-382-36626-3

Copyright © 2005, Pearson Education, Inc.

4 5 6 7 8 9 10 V039 09 08 07 06 05

Program Authors

Jane Beethoven

Susan Brumfield

Patricia Shehan Campbell

David N. Connors

Robert A. Duke

Judith A. Jellison

Rita Klinger

Rochelle Mann

Hunter C. March

Nan L. McDonald

Marvelene C. Moore

Mary Palmer

Konnie Saliba

Will Schmid

Carol Scott-Kassner

Mary E. Shamrock

Sandra L. Stauffer

Judith Thomas

Jill Trinka

Resource Book Contributing Authors

Jane Beethoven	Activity Masters
Susan Brumfield	Music Reading Worksheets Music Reading Practice
David N. Connors	Orff
Alice-Ann Darrow	Signing
Robert A. Duke	Assessment
Martha F. Hilley	Keyboard
Debbie Burgoon Hines	Pronunciation Practice Guides
Judith A. Jellison	Assessment
Rita Klinger	Music Reading Worksheets Music Reading Practice
Shirley Lacroix	Recorder
Rochelle Mann	Music Reading Worksheets Music Reading Practice
Konnie Saliba	Orff
Julie K. Scott	Orff Recorder
Judith Thomas	Orff
Jill Trinka	Music Reading Worksheets Music Reading Practice
CP Language Institute	Pronunciation Practice Guides

Master Table of Contents

PRONUNCIATION PRACTICE GUIDES

Recorded Pronunciation Practice tracks are provided in the CD package.

Table of Contents

© PEARSON EDUCATION, INC.

PRONUNCIATION PRACTICE 1

Gakavik (The Partridge)

Folk Song from Armenia

Phrase
① *A-rev paats-vedz*
ah-rehv pahts-vehdz

② *tugh am be-ren,*
toohkh ahm beh-rehn,

③ *ga-kav te-rav*
gah-kahv teh-rahv

④ *ga-nach sa-ren.*
gah-nahkh tsah-rehn.

⑤ *Ga-nach sa-ren*
gah-nahkh tsah-rehn

⑥ *sa-ri dze-ren,*
sah-ree tzeh-rehn,

⑦ *pa-rev pe-rav*
pah-rehv peh-rahv

⑧ *dza-ghik-ne-ren:*
tzah-gihkh-neh-rehn:

⑨ *Si-rov-nig, si-rov-nig,*
see-roo-nihgh, see-roo-nihgh,

⑩ *si-rov-nig, nakh-shoun*
see-roo-nihgh, nahkh-shoon

⑪ *ga-ka-vik.*
gah-kah-veek.

Grade 4, Teacher Edition, page 14

● PRONUNCIATION PRACTICE 2

Tsuki (The Moon)

School Song from Japan

Verse 1

Phrase ① *De-ta, de-ta, tsu-ki ga*
deh-tah, deh-tah, tsoo-kee gah

② *Ma-ru-i ma-ru-i ma-n-ma-ru-i,*
mah-roo-ee mah-roo-ee mah-(n)-mah-roo-ee,

③ *Bo-n-no yo-na tsu-ki ga.*
boh-(n)-noh yoh-nah, tsoo-kee gah.

Verse 2

Phrase ① *Ka-ku, re-ta ku-mo-ni,*
kah-koo, reh-tah koo-moh-nyee,

② *ku-roi, ku-roi ma-ku-roi,*
koo-roh_ee, koo-roh_ee mah-koo-roh_ee,

③ *Su-mi-no yo-na ku-mo-ni.*
soo-mee-noh yoh-nah, koo-moh-nyee.

PRONUNCIATION PRACTICE 3

Sonando

Words and Music by Peter Terrace

Phrase ① *So-nan-do*
soh-nahn-doh

② *pa-ra bai-lar,*
pah-rah bI-lahr,

③ *Go-za*
goh-tsah

④ *mi cha-cha-cha.*
mee chah-chah-chah.

⑤ *Lle-ga-ré Ma-rí-a, lle-ga-ré.*
djeh-gah-reh mah-ree-ah, djeh-gah-reh.

Pronunciation Practice 4

Hashewie (Going 'Round)

Folk Song from Eritrea, Africa

Phrase

① *Ha-shew-i-e Shew-i-e*
hah-sheh-wee-eh sheh-wee-eh

② *Ha-shew-i-e Shew-i-e*
hah-sheh-wee-eh sheh-wee-eh

③ *Ha-shew-i-e Shew-i-e*
hah-sheh-wee-eh sheh-wee-eh

④ *Bi-ha-de ha-bir-na Shew-i-e*
bee-hah-deh hah-beerr-nah sheh-wee-eh

⑤ *Ha-shew-ie‿e-na-bel-na Shew-i-e*
hah-sheh-wee‿eh-nah-behl-nah sheh-wee-eh

⑥ *A-lem kit-fel-to Shew-i-e*
ah-lehm kiht-fehl-toh sheh-wee-eh

⑦ *Ku-lu-me-nin-et-na Shew-i-e*
koo-loo-meh-nihn-eht-nah sheh-wee-eh

⑧ *Ha-shew-i-e ni-bel Shew-i-e*
hah-sheh-wee-eh nee-behl sheh-wee-eh

⑨ *Nef́-lit-a-di-na Shew-i-e*
nehf-lih-tah-dih-nah sheh-wee-eh

⑩ *Bi-ha-de ha-bir-na Shew-i-e.*
bee-hah-deh hah-beerr-nah sheh-wee-eh.

PRONUNCIATION PRACTICE 5

Riqui rán

Folk Song from Latin America

Verse 1

Phrase ① *A-se-rrín, a-se-rrán. Los ma-de-ros de San Juan*
ah-seh-rreen, ah-seh-rrahn. lohs mah-deh-rohs deh sahn hwahn

② *co-men que-so, co-men pan.*
koh-mehn keh-soh, koh-mehn pahn.

③ *Los de Ri-que, al-fe-ñi-que;*
lohs deh ree-keh, ahl-feh-nyee-keh;

④ *los de Ro-que, al-fon-do-que,*
lohs deh roh-keh, ahl-fohn-doh-keh,

⑤ *Ri-qui, ri-que, ri-qui rán.*
ree-kee, ree-keh, ree-kee rahn.

Verse 2

Phrase ① *A-se-rrín, a-se-rrán. Los a-be-jas vie-nen, van;*
ah-seh-rreen, ah-seh-rrahn. lohs ah-beh-has vyeh-nehn, vahn;

② *Miel la-bo-ran pa-ra_el pan.*
myehl lah-boh-rahn pah-rah_ehl pahn.

③ *Li-ban flo-res las de Ri-que*
lee-bahn floh-rehs lahs deh ree-keh

④ *cual al-mi-bar de_al-fe-ñi-que,*
kwahl ahl-mee-bahr deh_ahl-feh-nyee-keh,

⑤ *Y_el pa-nal de los de Ro-que*
yehl pah-nahl deh lohs deh roh-keh

⑥ *se pa-re-ce_a_un al-fon-do-que.*
seh pah-reh-seh_ah_oon ahl-fohn-doh-keh.

⑦ *Ri-qui, ri-que, ri-qui rán.*
ree-kee, ree-keh, ree-kee rahn.

A-6

PRONUNCIATION PRACTICE 5 (CONTINUED)

Verse 3

Phrase ① *A-se-rrín, a-se-rrán. Los chi-qui-llos. ¿Dón-de_es-tán?*
ah-seh-rreen, ah-seh-rrahn. lohs chee-kee-djohs. dawn-dehs-tahn?

② *To-dos a dor-mir se van.*
toh-dohs ah dohr-meer seh vahn.

③ *So-ña-rán con al-fe-ñi-que*
so-nyah-rrahn kohn ahl-feh-nyee-keh

④ *co-mo sue-ñan los de Ri-que,*
koh-moh sweh-nyahn lohs deh ree-keh,

⑤ *Y ma-ña-na_un al-fon-do-que*
ee mah-nyah-nah_oon ahl-fohn-doh-keh

⑥ *co-me-rán con los de Ro-que.*
koh-meh-rrrahn kohn lohs deh roh-keh.

⑦ *Ri-qui, ri-que, ri-qui rán.*
ree-kee, ree-keh, ree-kee rahn.

PRONUNCIATION PRACTICE 6

Eh, cumpari! (Hey, Buddy!)

*Words and Music by
Julius La Rosa and Archie Bleyer*

Phrase ① *Eh, cum-pa-ri!*
eh, koom-pah-ree!

② *Ci vo´ su-na-ri.*
chee voh soo-nah-ree.

③ *Chi si so-na*
kee see soh-nah

④ *´U fris-ca-le-ttu?*
oo frees-kah-leh-too?

⑤ *´U sax-o-fo-na?*
oo sahks-oh-foh-nah?

⑥ *´u man-du-li-nu?*
oo mahn-doo-lee-noo?

⑦ *´U vi-u-li-nu?*
oo vee-oo-lee-noo?

⑧ *A la trum-bet-ta?*
ah lah troom-beht-tah?

⑨ *A la trom-bo-na?*
ah lah trohm-boh-nah?

⑩ *E co-mu si so-na*
eh koh-moo see soh-nah

⑪ *´u fris-ca-let-tu?*
oo frees-kah-leh-too?

⑫ *´U sax-o-fo-na?*
oo sahks-oh-foh-nah?

PRONUNCIATION PRACTICE 6 (CONTINUED)

⑬ *´u man-du-li-nu?*
oo mahn-doo-lee-noo?

⑭ *'U vi-u-li-nu?*
oo vee-oo-lee-noo?

⑮ *A la trum-bet-ta?*
ah lah troom-beht-tah?

⑯ *A la trom-bo-na?*
ah lah trohm-boh-nah?

Last ending
Phrase ① *´u fris-ca-le-tt'e ti-pi-ti ti-pi-ti-ta.*
oo frees-kah-leh-teh tih-pih-tih tih-pih-tih-tah.

PRONUNCIATION PRACTICE 7

Hey, m'tswa-la

Folk Song from Africa

Phrase ① *Hey, m'tswa-la,*
heh, mtswah-lah,

② *ne-ye ti-pa sa-me tswa-la.*
neh-yeh tee-peh sah-meh tswah-lah.

PRONUNCIATION PRACTICE 8

Ōsamu kosamu (Biting Wind)

Folk Song from Japan

Part 1

Phrase ① *Ō-sa-mu, ko-sa-mu,*
oh-sah-moo, koh-sah-moo,

② *na-n to it-te*
nah-(n) toh eet-teh

③ *na-i-te-ki-ta?*
nah-ee-teh-kee-tah?

④ *Ō-sa-mu, ko-sa-mu.*
oh-sah-moo, koh-sah-moo.

Part 2

Phrase ① *Ya-ma-ka-ra ko-zoo ga*
yah-mah-kah-rah koh-tzoh gah

② *na-i-te-ki-ta;*
nah-ee-teh-kee-tah;

③ *"Sa-mu-i to it-te*
sah-moo-ee toh eet-teh

④ *na-i-te-ki-ta!"*
na-ee-teh-kee-tah!

⑤ *Ko-sa-mu.*
koh-sah-moo.

© PEARSON EDUCATION, INC.

PRONUNCIATION PRACTICE 9

T'hola, t'hola (Softly, Softly)

Folk Song from South Africa

Verse 1

Phrase
① *T'ho-la, t'ho-la ngoa-na-me;*
too-lah, too-lahn gwah-nah-meh;

② *T'ho-la, t'ho-la ngoa-na-me,*
too-lah, too-lahn gwah-nah-meh,

③ *Li pe-re se-ra peng.*
dee peh-reh see-rah pehng.

④ *Ra-peng sa-ma ha-pu.*
rah-pehng sah-mah hah-poo.

⑤ *Ei-tsa li lo tse-la*
eh_ee-tsah dee loh tseh-lah

⑥ *tsa ea-ngoa-na-me,*
tsah ee_ahn-gwah-nah-meh,

⑦ *E pu-tsoa ea khoa-ha mo*
eh poo-tswoh_ah eh_ah hkhwoh_ah-hah moh

⑧ *ko-ko Hon-goa-na-me*
koh-koh hohn-gwah-nah-meh

⑨ *E-i, e-i-ngoa-na-me,*
eh-yee, eh-yeen-gwah-nah-meh,

⑩ *E-i, e-i-ngoa-na-me.*
eh-yee, eh-yeen-gwah-nah-meh.

⑪ *Ha le so bone kon-ko-ti,*
hah lee see bohn kohn-koh-tee,

⑫ *Ha le so bone kon-ko-ti,*
hah lee see bohn kohn-koh-tee,

⑬ *T'ho-lá, t'ho-la ngoa-na-me,*
too-lah, too-lahn gwah-nah-meh,

⑭ *T'ho-la, t'ho-la ngoa-na-me.*
too-lah, too-lahn gwah-nah-meh.

PRONUNCIATION PRACTICE 10

Ala Da' lona

Arabic Folk Song

Verse 1

Phrase ① *A-la Da'-lo-na,*
ah-lah dah-loh-nah,

② *A-la Da'-lo-na,*
ah-lah dah-loh-nah,

③ *Hi-war shi-ma-li*
how-wahr shee-mah-lee

④ *gha-yar ih-lo-na.*
gwah-ee_yahr ee loo nah.

⑤ *Ma-ba-di i-mi*
mah-bah-dee ee-mee

⑥ *ma-ba-di ba-yi;*
mah-bah-dee bah-yee;

⑦ *Ba-di ha-bi-bi*
bah-dee hah-bee-bee

⑧ *as-mar ih-lo-na.*
hahs-mahr ih-loo-nah.

Grade 4, Teacher Edition, page 136

PRONUNCIATION PRACTICE 11

Canción de cuna (Cradle Song)

Folk Song from Latin America

Phrase ① *Duer-me pron-to, ni-ño mí-o,*
dwehr-meh prohn-toh, nee-nyoh mee-oh,

② *Duer-me pron-to_y sin llo-rar.*
dwehr-meh prohn-toh_ee seen yoh-rahr.

③ *Que_es-tás en los bra-zos de tu*
keh_ehs-tahs ehn lohs brah-zohs deh too

④ *ma-dre, que te va_a can-tar.*
mah-dreh, keh teh vah kahn-tahr.

© PEARSON EDUCATION, INC.

Cantando mentíras (Singing Tall Tales)

Folk Song from Latin America

Verse 1

Phrase ① *A-ho-ra que_es-ta-mos des-pa-cio,*
ah-oh-rah kehs-tah-mohs dehs-pah-see-oh,

② *Va-mos a can-tar men-tí-ras.*
vah-mohs ah kahn-tahr mehn-tee-rahs.

③ *Por el rí-o van las lie-bres,*
pohr ehl rree-oh vahn lahs lee_eh-brehs,

④ *Por el mon-te las an-gui-las.*
pohr ehl mohn-teh lahs ahn-gee-lahs.

Verse 2

Phrase ① *Los pe-rru-cos po-nen hue-vos,*
lohs peh-rroo-kohs poh-nehn hweh-vohs,

② *Las ga-lli-nas a la-drar,*
lahs gah-yee-nahs ah lah-drahr,

③ *Y_a los sa-pos cre-cen co-las,*
ee_ah los sah-pohs kreh-sehn koh-lahs,

④ *Por-que no sa-ben na-dar.*
pohr-keh noh sah-behn nah-dahr.

Grade 4, Teacher Edition, page 146

PRONUNCIATION PRACTICE 13

Ode to Joy

Words by Friedrich Schiller
Music by Ludwig van Beethoven

Phrase ① *Freu-de, schön-*er Göt-ter-fun-ken,*
fraw_ee-deh, shuh(r)n-ehr guh(r)t-tehr-foon-kehn,

② *Toch-ter aus E-ly-si-um,*
tohk-tehr ows** eh-lee-see-oom,

③ *wir be-tre-ten feu-er-trunk-en,*
veer beh-treh-tehn faw_ee-ehr-troonk-ehn,

④ *Himm-li-sche, dein Hei-lig-tum!*
heem-lih-sheh, dIn hI-lihg-toom!

⑤ *Dei-ne Zau-ber bin-den wie-der,*
dI-neh tsow-behr bihn-dehn vee-dehr,

⑥ *was die Mo-de streng ge-teilt;*
vahs dee moh-deh shtreng geh-tIlt;

⑦ *al-le Men-schen wer-den Brü-der,*
ahl-leh mehn-shehn vehr-dehn broo(r)-dehr,

⑧ *wo dein sanf-ter Flü-gel weilt.*
voh dIn sahnf-tehr floo(r)-gehl vIlt.

  * Sing the preceding vowel while shaping the mouth as if to sing an (r).
** ow: as in "pow"

Santa Clara

Folk Song from the Philippines

Verse

Phrase ① *San-ta Cla-ra,*
sahn-tah klah-rahng,

② *pi-nung pi-no*
pee-nuhng pee-noh

③ *Ang pa-nga-ko*
ahng pah-nah-koh

④ *ko ay ga-ni-to.*
koh ah‿ee gah-nee-toh.

⑤ *Pag-da-ting ko po*
pahg-dah-teeng koh poh

⑥ *sa U-ban-do.*
sah oo-bahn-doh.

⑦ *Ay mag-sa-sa-yaw*
ah‿ee mahg-sah-sah-yah‿ow

⑧ *ng pan-dang-go.*
nuhng pahn-dahng-goh.

Refrain

Phrase ① *A-ru-ray, a-ra-ru-ray,*
ah-roo-rah‿ee, ah-rah-ruh-rah‿ee,

② *Ang pa-nga-ko'y tu-tu-pa-rin.*
ahng pah-ngah-koh‿ee too-too-pah-reen.

③ *A-ru-ray, a-ra-ru-ray,*
ah-roo-rah‿ee, ah-rah-ruh-rah‿ee,

④ *Ang pa-nga-ko'y tu-tu-pa-rin.*
ahng pah-ngah-koh‿ee too-too-pah-reen.

● PRONUNCIATION PRACTICE 15

Doraji (Bluebells)

Folk Song from Korea

Phrase ① *Do-ra-ji, do-ra-ji,*
doh-rah-djee, doh-rah-djee,

② *pek do-ra-ji,*
pehk doh-rah-djee,

③ *Sim-sim san-chuh neh*
sheem-sheem sahn-choo neh

④ *pek do-ra-ji.*
pehk doh-rah-djee.

⑤ *Hahn du bu-ri-man*
hahn doo boo-ree-mahn

⑥ *keh-yuh-do*
keh-yuh-doh

⑦ *Teh kwang-chu-ri su-ri-sal sal*
teh kwahng-choo-ree shoo-ree-tsahl tsahl

⑧ *num-num-goo-na.*
nuhm-noom-goo-nah.

PRONUNCIATION PRACTICE 16

La Tarara

Folk Song from Spain

Refrain

Phrase ① *La Ta-ra-ra, sí, la Ta-ra-ra, no,*
lah tah-rah-rah, see, lah tah-rah-rah, noh,

② *La Ta-ra-ra, ma-dre, que la bai-lo yo.*
lah tah-rah-rah, mah-drreh, keh lah bah_ee-loh yoh.

Verse 1

Phrase ① *Tie-ne la Ta-ra-ra un jar-dín*
tyeh-neh lah tah-rah-rah oon hahrr-deen

② *de flo-res y me da, si quie-ro, siem-pre las me-jor-es.*
deh floh-rehs ee meh dah, see kee-eh-rroh, syehm-preh lahs meh-hohrr-ehs.

Verse 2

Phrase ① *Tie-ne la Ta-ra-ra un ces-to*
tyeh-neh lah tah-rah-rah oon sehs-toh

② *de fru-tas y me da, si quie-ro, siem-pre las ma-du-ras.*
deh froo-tahs ee meh dah, see kyeh-roh, syehm-preh lahs mah-doo-rrahs.

PRONUNCIATION PRACTICE 17

Los niños en España cantan
(In Spain, the Children Sing)

Folk Song from Mexico

Phrase   ①   *Los ni-ños en Es-pa-ña can-tan,*
                lohs nee-nyohs ehn ehs-pah-nyah kahn-tahn,

        ②   *can-tan en Ja-pón.*
                kahn-tahn ehn hah-pohn.

        ③   *Los pa-ja-ri-tos can-tan,*
                lohs pah-hah-ree-tohs kahn-tahn,

        ④   *can-tan to-dos su can-ción.*
                kahn-tahn toh-dohs soo kahn-see‿ohn.

PRONUNCIATION PRACTICE 18

El rancho grande (The Big Ranch)

Music by Silvano R. Ramos

Verse

Phrase ① *A-llá_en el ran-cho gran-de,*
ah-yah_ehn ehl rahn-choh grrahn-deh,

② *A-llá don-de vi-ví-a,*
ah-yah dohn-deh vee-vee-ah,

③ *Ha-bía_u-na ran-che-ri-ta,*
ah-bee_ah_oo-nah rahn-cheh-rree-tah,

④ *Que_a-le-gre me de-cí-a,*
keh_ah-leh-greh meh deh-see-ah,

⑤ *Que_a-le-gre me de-cí-a,*
keh_ah-leh-greh meh deh-see-ah,

Refrain

Phrase ① *Te voy ha-cer tus cal-zo-nes,*
teh voh_ee ah-sehr toos kahl-soh-nehs,

② *Co-mo los u-sa_el ran-che-ro;*
koh-moh lohs oo-sah_ehl rrahn-che-roh;

③ *Te los co-mien-zo de la-na,*
teh lohs koh-myehn-soh deh lah-nah,

④ *Te los a-ca-bo de cue-ro.*
teh lohs ah-kah-boh deh kweh-roh.

●PRONUNCIATION PRACTICE 19

Minka

Folk Song from Ukraine

Phrase ① *Tizh men-ye pid-ma-nu-la,*
tee_zhuh mehn-eh peed-mah-noo-lah,

② *tizh men-ye pid-ve-la.*
tee_zhuh mehn-eh peed-veh-lah.

③ *Tizh men-ye mo-lo-do-va,*
tee_zhuh mehn-eh moh-loh-doh-vah,

④ *zu-ma, ra-zu-ma zve-la.*
tzoo-mah, ehz_roh-zoo-moo zhveh-lah.

⑤ *Tizh men-ye pid-ma-nu-la,*
tee_zhuh mehn-eh peed-mah-noo-lah,

⑥ *tizh men-ye pid-ve-la.*
tee_zhuh mehn-eh peed-veh-lah.

⑦ *Tizh men-ye mo-lo-do-va,*
tee_zhuh mehn-eh moh-loh-doh-vah,

⑧ *zu-ma, ra-zu-ma zve-la.*
tzoo-mah, ehz_roh-zoo-moo zhveh-lah.

Thula, thula, ngoana
(Sleep, Sleep, Baby)

*Folk Song from the Lesotho Region
of South Africa*

Phrase ① *Thula, thula, ngoa-na,*
         too-lah, too-lah, ngwah-nah,

     ② *thula, thula, ngoa-na,*
         too-lah, too-lah, ngwah-nah,

     ③ *Thula, thula, ngoa-na,*
         too-lah, too-lah, ngwah-nah,

     ④ *thula, thula, ngoa-na.*
         too-lah, too-lah, ngwah-nah.

● PRONUNCIATION PRACTICE 21

Tengo, tengo, tengo (I Have Three Sheep)

Folk Song from New Mexico

Verse 1

Phrase ① *Ten-go, ten-go, ten-go,*
tehn-goh, tehn-goh, tehn-goh,

② *y tú no tie-nes na-da;*
ee too noh tee_eh-nehs nah-thah;

③ *Ten-go tres o-ve-jas,*
tehn-goh trehs oh-veh-hahs,

④ *a-llá en la ca-ña-da.*
ah-djah ehn lah kah-nyah-dah.

Verse 2

● Phrase ① *U-na me da le-che,*
oo-nah meh dah leh-cheh,

② *y o-tra me da la-na;*
ee oh-trah meh dah lah-nah;

③ *Y_o-tra man-te-qui-lla,*
ee_oh-trah mahn-teh-kee-djah,

④ *¡Ay! Pa-ra la se-ma-na.*
ah_ee! pah-rah lah seh-mah-nah.

PRONUNCIATION PRACTICE 22

Tancovačka (Dancing)

Slovak Folk Song

Phrase ① *Tan-cuj, tan-cuj,*
tahn-tsoo‿ee, tahn-tsoo‿ee,

② *vy-krú-caj, vy-krú-caj,*
vee-kroo-tsah‿ee, vee-kroo-tsah‿ee,

③ *Len mi pie-cku*
lehn mee pyeh-tskoo

④ *ne-zrú-caj, ne-zrú-caj.*
nyeh-tzroo-tsah‿ee, nyeh-tzroo-tsah‿ee.

⑤ *Do-brá pie-cka*
doh-brah pyeh-tskah

⑥ *na zi-mu, na zi-mu,*
nah zee-moo, nah zee-moo,

⑦ *Ked´ ne-má-me*
kehdj nyeh-mah-meh

⑧ *pe-ri-nu, pe-ri-nu.*
peh-ree-noo, peh-ree-noo.

© Pearson Education, Inc.

●PRONUNCIATION PRACTICE 23

El borrego (The Lamb)

Folk Song from Mexico

Phrase ① *Se-ño-ra, su bo-rre-gui-to,*
seh-nyohr-ah, soo boh-rreh-ghee-toh,

② *me quie-re lle-var al rí-o,*
meh kee‿eh-reh djeh-vahr ahl ree-oh,

③ *y yo le di-go que no,*
ee djoh leh dee-goh keh noh,

④ *por-que me mue-ro de frí-o.*
pohr-keh meh mweh-roh deh free-oh.

⑤ *Sa-le la lin-da,*
sah-leh lah leen-dah,

⑥ *sa-le la fe-a,*
sah-leh lah feh-ah,

⑦ *y‿el bo-rre-gui-to*
ee‿yehl boh-rreh-ghee-toh

⑧ *con su za-le-a.*
kohn soo sah-leh-ah.

⑨ *To-pe que to-pe,*
toh-peh keh toh-peh,

⑩ *to-pe con e-lla.*
toh-peh kohn eh-djah.

⑪ *To-pe que to-pe,*
toh-peh keh toh-peh,

⑫ *to-pe con él.*
toh-peh kohn ehl.

PRONUNCIATION PRACTICE 24

Cielito lindo

Folk Song from Mexico

Verse 1

Phrase

① *De la sie-rra mo-re-na,*
deh lah syeh-rah moh-reh-nah,

② *Cie-li-to lin-do,*
syeh-lee-toh leen-doh,

③ *vie-nen ba-jan-do,*
vyeh-nehn bah-hahn-doh,

④ *Un par de‿o ji-tos ne-gros,*
oon pahr deh‿oh-hee-tohs
  neh-grohs,

⑤ *Cie-li-to lin-do,*
syeh-lee-toh leen-doh,

⑥ *de con-tra-ban-do.*
deh kohn-trah-bahn-doh.

Refrain

Phrase

① *Ay, ay, ay ay!*
I, yI, yI, yI!

② *Can-ta‿y no llo-res.*
kahn-tah‿ee noh yoh-rehs.

③ *Por-que can-tan-do se‿a-le-gran,*
pohr-keh kahn-tahn-doh seh‿ah
  -leh-grahn,

④ *Cie-li-to lin-do,*
syeh-lee-toh leen-doh,

⑤ *los co-ra-zo-nes.*
lohs koh-rah-soh-nehs.

Verse 2

Phrase

① *E-se lu-nar que tie-nes,*
eh-seh loo-nahr keh
  tyeh-nehs,

② *Cie-li-to lindo,*
syeh-lee-toh leen-doh,

③ *jun-tó‿a la bo-ca,*
hoon-twah lah boh-kah,

④ *No se lo des a na-die,*
noh seh loh des ah
  nah-dyeh,

⑤ *Cie-li-to lin-do,*
syeh-lee-toh leen-doh,

⑥ *que‿a mí me to-ca.*
keh‿ah mee meh
  toh-kah.

Refrain

●PRONUNCIATION PRACTICE 25

Corrido de Kansas (Kansas *Corrido*)

Folk Song from Mexico

Verse 1

Phrase ① *Cuan-do sa-li-mos pa' Kan-sas*
kwahn-doh sah-lee-mohs pah kahn-sahs

② *Con u-na gran-de par-ti-da,*
kohn oo-nah grahn-deh pahr-tee-dah,

③ *Nos de-cí-a⁀el ca-po-ral:*
nohs deh-see-ah⁀ehl kah-poh-rahl:

④ *"No cuen-to ni con mi vi-da."*
noh kwehn-toh nee kohn mee vee-dah.

Verse 2

Phrase ① *Quin-ien-tos no-vi-llos er-an*
kee-nee⁀ehn-tohs noh-vee-djohs eh-rahn

② *Pe-ro to-dos muy li-via-nos,*
peh-roh toh-dohs moo⁀ee lee-vee⁀ah-nohs,

③ *No los po-día-mos re-par-ar*
noh lohs poh-dee⁀ah-mohs reh-pah-rahrr

④ *Sien-do trein-ta mex-i-ca-nos.*
see-ehn-doh trehn-tah meh-hee-kah-nohs.

Verse 3

Phrase ① *Cuan-do di-mos vis-ta⁀a Kan-sas*
kwahn-doh dee-mohs vee-stah⁀ah kahn-sahs

② *Er-a pu-ri-ti-to co-rrer,*
eh-rah poo-ree-tee-toh koh-rrehr,

③ *Er-an los ca-mi-nos lar-gos,*
eh-rahn lohs kah-mee-nohs lahr-gohs,

④ *Y pen-sa-ba yo en vol-ver.*
ee pehn-sah-bah djoh ehn vohl-vehr.

PRONUNCIATION PRACTICE 26

Farewell to the Warriors

Native American Song of the Chippewa

Phrase ① *Um-be a-ni-ma-djag*
           oom-beh ah-nee-mah-dyagh

    ② *wa-su-gi-di-zha-min,*
        wah-soo-djee-dee-zhah-meen,

    ③ *ya wi a ya wi a*
        yah wee ah yah wee ah

    ④ *ya ya wi a ya wi a.*
        yah yah wee ah yah wee ah.

● PRONUNCIATION PRACTICE 27

Ai Dunaiĭ moy (Ah, My Merry Dunaii)

Folk Song from Russia

Phrase ① *U vo-rot, vo-rot, vo-rot,*
oh vah-roht, vah-roht, vah-roht,

② *Da a vo-rot ba-tyush-ki-nykh,*
dah ah vah-roht bah-tyoosh-kee-nyeekh,

③ *Ai, Dun-aiĭ moy, Du-naiĭ,*
ah‿ee, doo-na‿hee mo‿hee, doo-na‿hee,

④ *Ai, ves-yo-lyi Du-naiĭ.*
ah‿ee, vee-syoh-lyee doo-na‿hee.

⑤ *Ra-zy-gra-il-sya re-bya-ta,*
rah-zgew-lyah-lee-syah reh-bee‿yah-tuh,

⑥ *ras-po-te-shi-lis,*
rahs-poh-teh-shee-lees,

⑦ *Ai, Du-naiĭ moy, Du-naiĭ,*
ah‿ee, doo-na‿hee mo‿hee, doo-na‿hee,

⑧ *Ai, ve-syo-lyi Du-naiĭ.*
ah‿ee, vee-syoh-lyee doo-na‿hee.

Beriozka (The Birch Tree)

Folk Song from Russia

Verse 1

Phrase ① *Va pa-lye bi-ryo ziny-ka sto-ya-la*
vah pah-leh bih-rryoh zihn_yuh-kah stah-yah-lah

② *Vo pa-lye kud-rya-va-ya sto-ya-la*
vah pah-leh kood-ryah-vah-yah stah-yah-lah

③ *Lyu-li lyu-li sta-ya-la*
loo-lee-loo-lee stah-yah-lah

④ *Lyu-li lyu-li sta-ya-la.*
loo-lee-loo-lee stah-yah-lah.

Verse 2

Phrase ① *Nye-ka-mu bi-ryo-zu za-la-ma-ti*
nyeh-kah-moo bee-ryoh-zoo zah-lah-mah-tee

② *Nye-ka-mu kud-rya-vu za-chi-pa-ti*
nyeh-kah-moo kood-ryah-voo zah-chee-pah-tee

③ *Lyu-li lyu-li za-la-ma-ti*
loo-lee-loo-lee zah-lah-mah-tee

④ *Lyu-li lyu-li za-chi-pa-ti.*
loo-lee-loo-lee zah-chee-pah-tee.

Verse 3

Phrase ① *Kak pay-du ya vlyes pa-gu-lya yu*
kahk pah_ee-doo yah vlyehs pah-goo-lyah yoo

② *bye-lu-yu bi-ryo-zu za-la-ma-yu*
byeh-loo-yoo bee-ryoh-zoo zah-lah-mah-yoo

Grade 4, Teacher Edition, page 294

PRONUNCIATION PRACTICE 28 (CONTINUED)

③ *Lyu-li lyu-li pa-gu-lya-yu*
loo-lee-loo-lee pah-goo-lyah-yoo

④ *Lyu-li lyu-li za-la-ma-yu.*
loo-lee loo-lee zah-lah-mah-yoo.

Verse 4

Phrase ① *Srez-hu s be-ryo-zu tree pru-toch-ka*
sreez-yoo ihs beh-rryoh-zoo tree proo-tohch-kah

② *Sdye-la-yu sye-bye ya tree gu-doch-ka*
sdee-luh-yoo syeh-byeh yeh tree goo-dohch-kah

③ *Lyu-li lyu-li tree pru-toch-ka*
loo-lee-loo-lee tree proo-tohch-kah

④ *Lyu-li lyu-li tree gu-doch-ka.*
loo-lee-loo-lee tree goo-dohch-kah.

PRONUNCIATION PRACTICE 29

Tina singu

Folk Song from South Africa

Phrase ① *Ti-na sing-u la-lu-vu tae-a*
tee-nah seeng-oom leh-loh-voh tah_ee-yoh

② *Wat-sha, wat-sha, wat-sha,*
waht-chah, waht-chah, waht-chah,

③ *Ti-na, Ti-na sing-u le-lu-vu_tae-o,*
tee-nah, tee-nah seeng-oom leh-loh-voh_tah_ee-yoh,

④ *wat-sha, wat-sha, wat-sha.*
waht-chah, waht-chah, waht-chah.

PRONUNCIATION PRACTICE 30

La raspa

Folk Song from Mexico

Phrase ① *La ras-pa yo bai-lé*
lah rahs-pah yoh bah_ee-leh

② *al de-re-cho y_al re-vés.*
ahl deh-reh-choh yahl reh-vehs.

③ *Si quie-res tú bai-lar,*
see kyeh-rehs too bah_ee-lahr,

④ *em-pie-za_a mo-ver los pies.*
ehm-pyeh-sah moo-vehr lohs pyehs.

⑤ *Brin-ca, brin-ca, brin-ca tam-bién,*
brin-kah, brin-kah, brin-kah tahm-byehn,

⑥ *mue-ve, mue-ve mu-cho los pies.*
mweh-veh, mweh-veh moo-choh lohs pyehs.

⑦ *Que la ras-pa vas a bai-lar*
keh lah rahs-pah vahs ah bah_ee-lahr

⑧ *al de-re-cho y al re-vés.*
ahl deh-reh-choh yahl reh-vehs.

⑨ *Si quie-res tú bai-lar*
see kyeh-rehs too bah_ee-lahr

⑩ *la ras-pa co-mo yo,*
lah rahs-pah koh-moh yoh,

⑪ *Me tie-nes que se-guir*
meh tyeh-nehs keh sah-gheer

⑫ *al de-re-cho y_al re-vés.*
ahl deh-reh-choh yahl reh-vehs.

⑬ *La ras-pa yo bai-lé*
lah rahs-pah yoh bah_ee-leh

⑭ *al de-re-cho-y_al re-vés.*
ahl deh-reh-choh yahl reh-vehs.

⑮ *Si quie-res tú bai-lar,*
see kyeh-rehs too bah_ee-lahr,

⑯ *em-pie-za_a amo-ver los pies.*
ehm-pyeh-sah moo-vehr lohs pyehs.

Grade 4, Teacher Edition, page 302

PRONUNCIATION PRACTICE 31

Bogando a la luz del sol (Rowing Toward the Sunlight)

Folk Song from Venezuela

Melody

Phrase ① *So-plan las bri-sas*
soh-plahn lahs bree-sahs

② *de la ma-ña-na,*
deh lah mah-nyah-nah,

③ *Ri-zan-do⌣el la-go*
ree-sahn-doh⌣ehl lah-goh

④ *mur-mu-ra-dor,*
moorr-moo-rah-dohrr,

⑤ *Y por o-rien-te*
ee pohr oh-ryehn-teh

⑥ *su faz a-so-ma*
soo fahs ah-soh-mah

⑦ *Cual ra-ro⌣in-cen-dio*
kwahl rrah-roh⌣een-sehn-dyoh

⑧ *la luz del sol.*
lah loos dehl sohl.

⑨ *Y por o-rien-te*
ee pohr oh-ryehn-teh

⑩ *su faz a-so-ma*
soo fahs ah-soh-mah

⑪ *Cual ra-ro⌣in-cen-dio*
kwahl rrah-roh⌣een-sehn-dyoh

⑫ *la luz del sol.*
lah loos dehl sohl.

Countermelody

Phrase ① *So-plan las bri-sas*
soh-plahn lahs bree-sahs

② *de la ma-ña-na,*
deh lah mah-nyah-nah,

③ *Y por o-rien-te*
ee pohr oh-ryehn-teh

④ *su faz a-so-ma.*
soo fahs ah-soh-mah.

⑤ *Y por o-rien-te*
ee pohr oh-ryehn-teh

⑥ *su faz a-so-ma*
soo fahs ah-soh-mah

⑦ *Cual ra-ro⌣in-cen-dio*
kwahl rah-roh⌣een-sehn-dyoh

⑧ *la luz del sol.*
lah loos dehl sohl.

PRONUNCIATION PRACTICE 32

Sakura

Folk Song from Japan

Phrase ① *Sa-ku-ra, sa-ku-ra,*
sah-koo-rah, sah-koo-rah,

② *Ya-yo i no so-ra wa*
yah-yoh ee noh soh-rah wah

③ *Me-wa-ta-su ka-gi-ri*
mee-wah-tah-soo kah-gee-rree

④ *Ka-su-me ka ku-mo-ka,*
kah-soo-mee kah koo-moh-kah,

⑤ *Ni-o-i zo i-zu-ru;*
nee-hoh-ee tzoh ee-tzoo-roo;

⑥ *i-za-ya, i-za-ya,*
ee-tzah-yah, ee-tzah-yah,

⑦ *Mi ni yu-kan.*
mee nee yoo-kah(n).

PRONUNCIATION PRACTICE 33

Feng yang hua gu (*Feng Yang* Song)

Folk Song from China

Phrase ① *Zuo shou luo,*
tzwoh show loo_wow,

② *you shou gu,*
yoh show goo,

③ *Shou na zhe luo gu*
show nah juh loo_wow goo

④ *lai chang ge!*
lah_ee chahng guh!

⑤ *Bie di ge er*
bee_yeh dee guh uhr

⑥ *wo ye bu hui chang,*
wow yeh boo hweh_ee chahng,

⑦ *Zhi hui chang ge Feng Yang ge.*
jihr hweh_ee chahng guh fuhng yahng guh.

⑧ *Feng la, feng yang*
fuhng lah, fuhng yahng

⑨ *ge er lai,*
guh uhr lah_ee,

⑩ *Der lang dang piao yi piao,*
d'rrrr luhng-duhng pyow yee pyow,

⑪ *Der lang dang piao yi piao,*
d'rrrr luhng-duhng pyow yee pyow,

⑫ *Der piao! Der piao!*
d'rrrr pyow! d'rrrr pyow!

⑬ *Der piao der piao piao ye der piao piao piao yi piao!*
d'rrrr pyow d'rrrr pyow pyow yee
d'rrrr pyow pyow pyow yee
pyow!

Xiao (Bamboo Flute)

Folk Song from China

Phrase ① *Yi geng zi zhu*
yee gawng dzuh joo

② *zhi miao miao;*
juh mee‿ow mee‿ow;

③ *Sung yu bao bao zuo guan xiao.*
sohng yuh bow bow tshoo‿oh gwahn shee‿ow.

④ *Xiao er dui zheng kou*
shee‿ow ehr dweh jehng koh

⑤ *Kou er dui zheng xiao;*
koh ehr dweh jehng shee‿ow;

⑥ *Xiao zhong chui chu*
shee‿ow juhng chweh choo

⑦ *shi xin diao;*
shee sheen dee‿ow;

⑧ *Xiao bao bao*
shee‿ow bow bow

⑨ *yi di yi di xue hui liao,*
yee dee yee dee shau wheh lee‿ow,

⑩ *Xiao bao bao*
shee‿ow bow bow

⑪ *Yi di yi di xue hui liao.*
yee dee yee dee shau wheh lee‿ow.

Grade 4, Teacher Edition, page 314

● PRONUNCIATION PRACTICE 35

Yibane amenu

Round from Israel

Phrase ① *Yi-ba-ne a-me-nu*
yee-bah-neh ah-meh-noo

② *b-´ar-tse-nu;*
buh-ahr-tzeh-noo;

③ *Yi-ba-ne a-me-nu*
yee-bah-neh ah-meh-noo

④ *b-´ar-tse-nu;*
buh-ahr-tzeh-noo;

⑤ *B-´ar-tse-nu, yi-ba-ne,*
buh-ahr-tzeh-noo, yee-bah-neh,

⑥ *B-´ar-tse-nu, yi-ba-ne,*
buh-ahr-tzeh-noo, yee-bah-neh,

⑦ *Yi-ba-ne, Yi-ba-ne.*
yee-bah-neh, yee-bah-neh.

⑧ *Yi-ba-ne, Yi-ba-ne.*
yee-bah-neh, yee-bah-neh.

PRONUNCIATION PRACTICE 36

Niu lang zhi nü
(The Cowherd and the Weaving Maid)

Folk Song from China

Verse 1

Phrase ① *Tiau tiau chien niu hsing,*
dzah-oh dzah-oh chee_ehn nyow sheeng,

② *jiau jiau hě han nü*
jee-ow jee-ow suh hahn new

③ *hsien hsien ien su shou*
shyeh-ehn shyehn yehn shoo shoh

④ *zha zha nong ji zhu*
dzah dzah nuhng jee dzhoo

⑤ *ing ing i hsuei jien*
eeng eeng ee shweh djee_ehn

⑥ *mu-o mu-o bu de ü.*
mwah-oh mwah-oh boo dah ew.

Verse 2

Phrase ① *Zhong zhru bu cheng zhang,*
tzhawng zhroo boo chehng dzahng,

② *chi ti lei zhru ü*
chee tee leh zhroo ew

③ *ne han ching chie chien*
nuh hahn cheeng chee-eh chee-ehn

④ *hsiang chü fu ji hsü*
shee_ahng chew foo jee shew

⑤ *ing ing i hsuei jien*
eeng eeng ee shweh djee_ehn

⑥ *mu-o mu-o bu de ü.*
mwah-oh mwah-oh boo dah ew.

Grade 4, Teacher Edition, page 335

PRONUNCIATION PRACTICE 37

Somos el barco (We Are the Boat)

Words and Music by Lorre Wyatt

Phrase ① *So-mos el bar-co,*
soh-mohs ehl bahr-koh,

② *So-mos el mar.*
soh-mohs ehl mahr.

③ *Yo na-ve-go en ti,*
yoh nah-veh-goh ehn tee,

④ *Tu na-ve-gas en mí.*
too nah-veh-gahs ehn mee.

PRONUNCIATION PRACTICE 38

Sailboat in the Sky

Folk Song from Korea

Phrase ① *Pu reun ha nul eun-ha su ha yan jjok bae ae,*
poo roon hah nuhl oon-hah soo hah yahn johk beh eh,

② *Gae su na mu han-na mu to kki han ma ri,*
geh soo nah moo hahn-nah moo toh kee hahn mah ree,

③ *Dot dae do ah ni dal go sat dae do up si,*
doht deh doh ah nee dahl goh sah deh doh oop see,

④ *Ga gi do jal do gahn da so-jjok na ra ro.*
gah ghee doh jahl doh gahn dah soh-johk nah rah roh.

PRONUNCIATION PRACTICE 39

Einini

Gaelic Folk Song

Part 1

Phrase ① *Ein-in-i, ein-in-i,*
eh_ee-nee-nee, eh_ee-nee-nee,

② *cod-al-ai-gi, cod-al-ai-gi,*
kohd-ahl-ee-gee, kohd-ahl-ee-gee,

③ *ein-in-i, ein-in-i,*
eh_ee-nee-nee, eh_ee-nee-nee,

④ *cod-al-ai-gi, cod-al-ai-gi.*
kohd-ahl-ee-gee, kohd-ahl-ee-gee.

⑤ *Cod-al-ai-gi, cod-al-ai-gi,*
kohd-ahl-ee-gee, kohd-ahl-ee-gee,

⑥ *cois an chlai am-uigh, cois an chlai am-uigh,*
kohsh uhn klee uhm-wee, kohsh uhn klee uhm-wee,

⑦ *cod-al-ai-gi, cod-al-ai-gi,*
kohd-ahl-ee-gee, kohd-ahl-ee-gee,

⑧ *cois an chlai am-uigh, cois an chlai am-uigh.*
kohsh uhn klee uhm-wee, kohsh uhn klee uhm-wee.

⑨ *Cod-al-ai-gi, cod-al-ai-gi,*
kohd-ahl-ee-gee, kohd-ahl-ee-gee,

⑩ *cois an chlai amuigh, cois an chlai amuigh.*
kohsh uhn klee uhm_wee, kohsh uhn klee uhm_wee.

Part 2
(Same as above)

Grade 4, Teacher Edition, page 391

● PRONUNCIATION PRACTICE 40

Sambalele

Folk Song from Brazil

Phrase ① *Sam-ba-le-le ta do-en-te,*
sahm-bah-lah-leh tah doh_ehn-chee,

② *tac-oa ca-be-ça que bra-da*
tah-kwah kah-beh-sah keh brah-dah

③ *Sam-ba-le-le pre-ci-sa-va*
sahm-bah-lah-leh preh-see-sah-vah

④ *de_u-mas de zoi-to lam-ba-das,*
djoo-mahsh dee zoh_ee-too lahm-bah-dahsh,

⑤ *Sam-ba-le-le ta do-en-te,*
sahm-bah-lah-leh tah doh_ehn-chee,

⑥ *ta coa ca-be-ça, que bra-da*
tah-kwah kah-beh-sah keh brah-dah

⑦ *Sam-ba-le-le pre-ci-sa-va*
sahm-bah-lah-leh preh-see-sah-vah

⑧ *de_u-mas de zoi-to lam-ba-das,*
djoo-mahsh dee zoh_ee-too lahm-bah-dahsh,

⑨ *Sam-ba sam-ba sam-ba-le-le*
sahm-bah sahm-bah sahm-bah-leh-leh

⑩ *Pi-sa-na ba-ra da sa-ia le-le!*
pee-sah-nah bah-hah dah sah-yoh leh-leh!

⑪ *Sam-ba sam-ba sam-ba-le-le!*
sahm-bah sahm-bah sahm-bah-leh-leh!

⑫ *Pi-sa-na bar-ra da sa-ia*
pee-sah-nah bah-hah dah sah-yah

Grade 4, Teacher Edition, page 397

⑬ *Ba-la-io meu bem, Ba-la-io sin-ha*
bah-lah-yoh meh_oh behm, bah-lah-yoh seen-yah

⑭ *ba-la-io do co-ra-ção*
bah-lah-yoh doo koh-rah-sow(n)*

⑮ *Mo-ça-que não tem ba-la-io sin-ha*
mah-sah-keh now tehn bah-lah-yoh see-yah

⑯ *bo-taa cos-tu-ra no chão.*
boh-tah kohs-too-rah noo show.*

⑰ *Ba-la-io meu bem, ba la-io sin-ha*
bah-lah-yoh meh_oh behm, bah-lah-yoh seen-yah

⑱ *ba-la-io do co-ra-ção*
bah-lah-yoh doo koh-rah-sow(n)*

⑲ *Mo-ça-que não tem ba-la-io sin-ha*
mah-sah-keh now tehn bah-lah-yoh seen-yah

⑳ *bo-taa cos-tu-ra no chão!*
boh-tah kohs-too-rah noo show!*

*ow: as in "cow"

PRONUNCIATION PRACTICE 41

A Merry Modal Christmas

La marche des rois

Carol from France

Phrase ① *Ce ma-tin,*
suh mah-tah(n),

② *J'ai ren-con-tré le train,*
zheh rah(n)-kohn-treh luh trah(n),

③ *De trois grands Rois*
duh twah grah(n) rwah

④ *qui al-laient en-voy-a-ge,*
kee ahl-leht ah(n)-voh-ah-zhuh,

⑤ *Ce ma-tin,*
suh mah-tah(n),

⑥ *J'ai ren-con-tré le train,*
zheh rah(n)-kohn-treh luh trah(n),

⑦ *De trois grands Rois*
duh twah grah(n) rwah

⑧ *des-sus le grand che-min.*
deh-soo luh grah(n)d shuh-mah(n).

⑨ *Tout char-gés d'or les sui-vant d'a-bord,*
too shahr-zheh dohr leh swee-vahnt dah-bohr,

⑩ *De grands guer-riers*
duh grah(n) geh-reeyehr

⑪ *et les gar-des du tré-sor,*
eh leh gahr-deh doo treh-sohr,

© PEARSON EDUCATION, INC.

⑫ *Tout char-gés d'or les sui-vant d'a-bord*
too shahr-zheh dohr leh swee-vahnt dah-bohr

⑬ *De grands guer-riers*
duh grah(n) geh-reeyehr

⑭ *a-vec leurs bou-cli-ers.*
ah-vehk luhr boo-klee-ehr.

Pat-a-pan

Words and Music by Bernard de la Monnoye

Verse 1

Phrase ① *Guil-lo, prends ton tam-bou-rin,*
gee-yoh, prahn tohn tahm-boh-rah(n),

② *Toi prends ta flú-te, Ro-bin;*
twah, prah(n) tah floo-tuh, roh-beh(n);

③ *Au son de cés in-stru-ments,*
oh soh(n) duh sehs een-stroo-mah(n),

④ *Tu-re-lu-re-lu, pat-a-pat-a-pan;*
too-ruh-loo-ruh-loo, pah-tah-pah-tah-pah(n);

⑤ *Au son de cés in-stru-ments,*
oh soh(n) duh sehs een-stroo-mah(n),

⑥ *Je di-rai No-ël gaie-ment.*
zhuh dee-reh noh-ehl geh-mah(n).

PRONUNCIATION PRACTICE 42

La copa de la vida (The Cup of Life)

Words and Music by Desmond Child and Robi Rosa

Verse 1

Phrase ① *Co-mo Cain y A-bel*
koh-moh kah_een ee ah-behl

② *es un par-ti-do cruel.*
ehs oon pahr-tee-thoh kroo_ehl.

③ *Tie-nes que pe-le-ar por un-a es-tre-lla*
tyeh-nehs keh peh-leh-ahrr pohr oo-nah ehs-treh-yah

④ *Con-si-gue con hon-or*
kohn-see-geh kohn oh-nohr

⑤ *la co-pa del a-mor.*
lah koh-pah dehl ah-mohrr.

⑥ *Pa-ra so-bre vi-vir y lu-char por e-lla*
pah-rah soh-breh vee-veer ee loo-chahr pohr eh-yah

⑦ *Lu-char por e-lla.*
loo-chahr pohr eh-yah.

Verse 2

Phrase ① *La vi-da es com-pe-ti-ción.*
lah vee-thah ehs kohm-peh-tee-syohn.

② *Hay que so-ñar, ser cam-pe-ón.*
ah_ee keh soh-nyahr, sehr kahm-peh-ohn.

③ *La co-pa es la ben-di-ción,*
lah koh-pah ehs lah behn-dee-syohn,

④ *la ga-na-rás, go, go, go.*
lah gah-nah-rahs, goh, goh, goh.

Refrain

Phrase ① *Uno, dos, tres, o-lé, o-lé, o-lé.*
oo_noh, dohs, trehs, oh-leh, oh-leh, oh-leh.

② *Un, deux, trois, Al-lez, al-lez, al-lez.*
uh(n) duh, twah, ah-leh, ah-leh, ah-leh.

© PEARSON EDUCATION, INC.

Shir l'shalom
(Hand in Hand—A Song for Peace)

Hebrew Words by Jacob Rotblitt
Music by Yair Rosenblum

Verse 1

Phrase ① *Tnu la-she-mesh la-a-lot,*
tnoo lah-sheh-mehsh lah-ah-loht,

② *la-bo-ker l'-ha-ir.*
luh-boh-kehr leh-hah-eer.

③ *Ha-za-kah she-ba-tfi-lot*
hah-zah-kah sheh-bah-t'fee-loht

④ *o-ta-nu lo tach zir.*
oh-tah-noo loh tah-khzihr.

⑤ *Mi a-sher ka-va ne-ro*
mee ah-sheer kah-vah neh-roh

⑥ *u-v'-a-far nit-man,*
oo-vuh-ah-fahr neet-mahn,

⑦ *Be-chi mar lo ya-i-ro*
beh-hkhee mahr loh yah-ee‿raw

⑧ *lo yach-zi-ro l'-chan.*
loh-yakh-zee-roh luh-hkhahn.

⑨ *Ish o-ta-nu lo ya-shiv*
eesh oh-tah-noo lah yah-sheev

⑩ *mi-bor tach-teet a-fel.*
mee-bohr tahkh-teet ah-fehl.

⑪ *Kan lo yo-i-lu lo shi-rey*
kahn loh yoh-ee-loo loh shee-reh

Grade 4, Teacher Edition, page 419

PRONUNCIATION PRACTICE 43 (CONTINUED)

⑫ *ha-ni-tsa-chon*
hah-nee-tzah-hkhohn

⑬ *v'-lo shi-rey ha-lel.*
vuh-loh shee-reh hah-lehl.

⑭ *La' chen rak shi-ru shir l'-sha-lom,*
lah hkhehn rahk shee-roo shihr lah-shah-lohm,

⑮ *al til-cha-shu tfi-la.*
ahl tee-lkha-shoo tfee-lah.

⑯ *La' chen rak shi-ru shir l'-sha-lom*
lah khehn rahk shee-roo shihr lah-shah-lohm

⑰ *bi-tse-a-kah g'do-lah!*
buh-tzah-ah-kah guh-doh-lah!

Verse 2

Phrase ① *Tnu la-she-mesh la-cha-dor*
tnoo lah-sheh-mehsh lah-hkhah-dohrr

② *mi-ba-'ad la-pra-chim.*
mee-bah-ahd lah-prah-hkheem.

③ *al ta-bi-tu l'-a-chor,*
ahl tah-bee-too leh-ah_hkhohrr,

④ *ha-ni-chu la-hol-chim.*
hah-nee-hkhoo lah-hkhohl-hkheem.

⑤ *Su ey-na-yim b'-tik-vah,*
suh-oo eh-nah-yeem buh-teek-vah,

⑥ *lo de-rech ka-va-not.*
loh deh-rehkh kah-vah-noht.

⑦ *Shi-ru shir la-a-ha-vah,*
shee-roo shihr lah-ah-hah-vah,

⑧ *v'-lo la-mil-cha-mot.*
vuh-loh lah-mihl-hkhah-moht.

⑨ *Al ta-gi-du yom ya-vo,*
ahl tah-gee-doo yohm yah-vaw,

⑩ *ha viy-u et ha-yom!*
hah-vee-oo eht hah-yohm!

⑪ *Ki lo-cha-lom hu. U-v'-chol*
kee lah-hkhah-lohm hoo. oo-vuh-hkhohl

⑫ *ha-ki-ka-rot ha-ri-u l'-sha-lom!*
hah-kee-kah-rawt hah-ree-oo lah-shah-lohm!

⑬ *La' chen rak shi-ru shir l'-sha-lom,*
lah hkhehn rahk shee-roo shihr lah-shah-lohm,

⑭ *al til-cha-shu tfi-la.*
ahl tee-lkha-shoo tfee-lah.

⑮ *La' chen rak shi ru shir l'-sha-lom*
lah hkhehn rahk shee-roo shihr lah-sha-lohm

⑯ *bi-tse-a-kah g'do-lah!*
buh-tzeh-ah-kah guh-doh-lah!

⑰ *g'do-lah!*
guh-doh-lah!

© PEARSON EDUCATION, INC.

PRONUNCIATION PRACTICE 44

Ocho kandelikas (Eight Little Candles)

Words and Music by Flory Jagoda

Verse 1

Phrase ① *Ha-nu-ka lin-da sta a-ki*
hah-noo-kah lihn-dah stah ah-kee

② *o-cho kan-de-las pa-ra mi.*
oh-choh kahn-deh-lahs pah-rah mee.

③ *Ha-nu-ka lin-da sta a-ki*
hah-noo-kah lihn-dah stah ah-kee

④ *o-cho kan-de-las pa-ra mi.*
oh-choh kahn-deh-lahs pah-rah mee.

Refrain

Phrase ① *u-na kan-de-li-ka, dos kan-de-li-kas,*
oo-nah kahn-deh-lee-kah, dohs kahn-deh-lee-kahs,

② *tres kan-de-li-kas, kuat-ro kan-de-li-kas,*
trrehs kahn-deh-lee-kahs, kwaht-rro kahn-deh-lee-kahs,

③ *sin-ko kan-de-li-kas, sej kan-de-li-kas,*
seen-koh kahn-deh-lee-kahs, sehdj kahn-deh-lee-kahs,

④ *sie-te kan-de-li-kas,*
see_eh-teh kahn-deh-lee-kahs,

⑤ *o-cho kan-de-las pa-ra mi.*
oh-choh kahn-deh-lahs pah-rah mee.

Verse 2

Phrase ① *Mu-chas fi-e-stas vo fa-zer*
moo-chahs fee-eh-stahs voh fah-zehrr

② *kan a-le-gri-as i pla-zer.*
kahn ah-leh-gree-ahs ee plah-zehrr.

③ *Mu-chas fi-e-stas vo fa-zer*
moo-chahs fee-eh-stahs voh fah-zehrr

④ *kon a-le-gri-as i pla-zer.*
kahn ah-leh-gree-ahs ee plah-zehrr.

Verse 3

Phrase ① *Los pas-te-li-kos vo ko-mer*
lahs pahs-teh-lee-kohs voh koh-mehrr

② *kon al-men-dri-kas i la myel.*
kohn ahl-mehn-drree-kahs ee lah myehl.

③ *Los pas-te-li-kos vo ko-mer*
lahs pahs-teh-lee-kohs voh koh-mehrr

④ *kon al-men-dri-kas i la myel.*
kohn ahl-mehn-drree-kahs ee lah myehl.

● PRONUNCIATION PRACTICE 45

Al quebrar la piñata (Piñata Song)

Christmas Song from Mexico

Phrase ① *En las no-ches de po-sa-das,*
ehn lahs noh-chehs deh poh-sah-dah,

② *La pi-ña-ta_es lo me-jor;*
lah peen-yah-tah_ehs loh meh-hohr;

③ *La ni-ña mas re-mil-ga-da*
lah neen-yah mahs reh-meel-gah-dah

④ *Se_al-bo-ro-ta con ar-dor.*
seh_ahl-boh-roh-tah kohn ahr-dohr.

⑤ *Da-le, da-le, da-le*
dah-leh, dah-leh, dah-leh

⑥ *no pier-das el ti-no.*
noh p'yehr-dahs ehl tee-noh.

⑦ *Que de la dis-tan-cia*
keh deh lah dee-stahn-s'yah

⑧ *se pier-de_el ca-mi-no.*
seh p'yehr-deh_ehl kah-mee-noh.

Dayenu (It Would Have Been Enough) *Jewish Passover Song*

Verse 1

Phrase

① *I-lu ho-tzi, ho-tzi-a-nu,*
ee-loo hoh-tzee, hoh-tzee-
yah-noo,

② *ho-tzi-a-nu mi-Mitz-ra-yim,*
hoh-tzee-yah-noo mee-mihtz-
rah-yihm,

③ *hoh-tzi-a-nu mi-Mitz-ra-yim,
da-ye-nu.*
hoh-tzee-yah-noo mee-mihtz-
rah-yeem, dah_ih-yehy-noo.

Refrain

Phrase

① *Da-da-ye-nu, da-da-ye-nu,*
dah_ih-dah_ih -yehy-noo,
dah_ih-dah_ih -yehy-noo,

② *da-da-ye-nu, da-ye-nu, da-ye-
nu, da-ye-nu.*
dah_ih-dah_ih-yehy-noo,
dah_ih-yehy-noo, dah_ih-
yehy-noo, dah_ih-yehy-noo.

③ *Da-da-ye-nu, da-da-ye-nu,*
dah_ih-dah_ih-yehy-noo,
dah_ih-dah_ih-yehy-noo,

④ *da-da-ye-nu, da-ye-nu, da-ye-nu.*
dah_ih-dah_ih-yehy-noo,
dah_ih-yehy-noo, dah_ih-
yehy-noo.

Verse 2

Phrase

① *I-lu na-tan na-tan lo-nu,*
ee-loo nah-tahn nah-tahn
lah-noo,

② *na-tan lo-nu et ha-Sha-bat,*
nah-tahn lah-noo eht hah-
shah-baht,

③ *na-tan lo-nu et ha-Sha-bat, da-
ye-nu.*
nah-tahn lah-noo eht hah-
shah-baht, dah_ih-yehy-noo.

Verse 3

Phrase

① *I-lu na-tan na-tan la-nu,*
ee-loo nah-tahn nah-tahn
lah-noo,

② *na-tan la-nu et ha-To-ra,*
nah-tahn lah-noo eht hah-
toh-rah,

③ *na-tan la-nu et ha-To-ra, da-
ye-nu.*
nah-tahn lah-noo eht hah-
toh-rah, dah_ih-yehy-noo.

PRONUNCIATION PRACTICE 47

Phonetic Pronunciation for Choral Singing of Non-English Songs

ah	as in father
ah_ee	as in light (diphthong; a long *ah* sound with a hint of *ee* at close)
aw	as in awe
eh_ee	as in day (diphthong; a long *eh* sound with a hint of *ee* at close)
b	as in button
ch	as in church
d	as in dad
dj	as in judge
ee	as in seed
eh	as in let
ew	used for French u (pronounce a bright *ee* and round the lips as if to whistle)
f	as in face
g	as in goat
h	as in hat
hkh	guttural, aspirant h of German, Hebrew ch, and Spanish j
ih	as in fit
I	as in light (a harsh *i* sound, where possible an *ah_ee* has been suggested for singing the I sound)
k	as in kite
l	as in let
ll	prolonged l sound
m	as in man
(m)	French nasal m, not articulated as a distinct letter but as an open nasal sound
n	as in note
(n)	French nasal n, not articulated as a distinct letter, but as an open nasal sound.
(ng)	as in sang (sometimes sounded as a prolonged nasal tone)
oh	as in tone
oo	as in spoon
ow	as in powder
p	as in pat
r	as in ran
(r)	as in turn (combined with another vowel sound in German)
rr	rolled r
rrrr	extended trilled r
s	as in song
t	as in tell
th	as in that
thh	as in feather
uh	as in up
v	as in van
w	as in way
wh	as in what
y	as in yes (not a vowel sound)
z	as in zone
zh	as in azure

Teacher Notes

ASSESSMENT
Table of Contents

ASSESSMENT

ASSESSMENT 1: UNIT 1

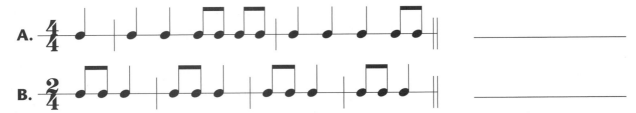

1. Which of these rhythm patterns is the beginning of *"Gakavik"*? Which is the beginning of "Soldier, Soldier"? Write the correct song titles next to the rhythm patterns.

A. _____

B. _____

2. Use ♩, ♫, and 𝄾 to **create** a rhythm pattern in duple meter that is eight beats long.

_____

Show What You Know!

Read the following melodies using pitch syllables.

1.

2.

3.

Look at the phrases above. How would you **identify** the tonal center of these phrases if the beginning were not marked with *do*?

_____

_____

Assessment 1: Unit 1 (continued)

Review, Assess, Perform, Create

What Do You Know?

1. Look at the notation for "*Tsuki*" on page 25. Then answer these questions.

  a. Where is *do* located in the music? _____

  b. Count all the notes named *so*. How many did you find? _____

  c. Do the same activity for the notes named *mi*, *re*, *la*, and *do*.

   mi _____   *re* _____   *la* _____   *do* _____

2. Match each dynamic symbol with the correct definition. Write the letter of your answer in the space provided.

  a. *mf*   ____ loud

  b. *p*   ____ gradually louder

  c. *mp*   ____ medium loud

  d. ▷   ____ soft

  e. *f*   ____ medium soft

  f. ◁   ____ gradually softer

ASSESSMENT 1: UNIT 1 (CONTINUED)

What Do You Hear? 1   **Vocal Timbre**

Listen to each example and describe the timbre, using at least three adjectives in your description. Write your answers below.

1. *Rain, Rain, Beautiful Rain*

_____

_____

2. *I Don't Want to Feel Like That*

_____

_____

3. *Nahandove*

_____

_____

4. *Sigit "Alash"*

_____

_____

Grade 4, Teacher Edition, page 42

● ASSESSMENT 1: UNIT 1 (CONTINUED)

What You Can Do

Create Dynamics

Create a dynamics roadmap to follow while you sing "Waitin' for the Light to Shine" on page 26. Remember that dynamics should express the feelings and mood of the song.

Move to the Beat

Use movement to show strong and weak beats while you sing "*Gakavik*" on page 14. With a partner, create work movements to perform as you sing "Haul Away, Joe" on page 13.

Read a Melody

Read the notation for *"Tsuki"* on page 25, using pitch syllables and hand signs. Then perform the song again with the words.

Create Textures

Divide into two groups and perform "Pay Me My Money Down," on page 38, in call-and-response style. Sing the song again with only a few students singing the call and the rest of the class singing the response. Create additional verses to the song and perform them as a solo caller while the rest of the class sings the responses.

ASSESSMENT

ASSESSMENT 2: UNIT 2

1. Clap and **perform** these rhythms using rhythm syllables. **Identify** the song.

2. Write your own rhythms in 4/4 meter. Use one example of syncopation and one rest.

Show What You Know!

1. Sing this melody using pitch syllables.

2. Now write the letter names for the pitches in the spaces provided above. **Play** the melody on a xylophone or keyboard.

3. Sing this melody using pitch syllables. Write the letter names below the notes. Then sing the notes using letter names and **play** the melody on recorder.

ASSESSMENT 2: UNIT 2 (CONTINUED)

Review, Assess, Perform, Create

What Do You Know?

1. Look at the notation for "Joe Turner Blues" on page 56. Find the time signature. How many beats are in each measure? _____

2. Name the title of a song in Unit 2 that has:

a. Three beats in each measure: _____

b. Two beats in each measure: _____

3. Reorder these musical terms for tempo from slowest to fastest. Use 1 for the slowest tempo and 5 for the fastest tempo.

_____ *andante*   _____ *presto*   _____ *adagio*   _____ *allegro*   _____ *moderato*

What Do You Hear? 2   Identifying Timbre

Listen to these instrumental excerpts. Identify the instrument or instruments you hear. Circle your answers.

1.	brass	strings	woodwinds
2.	brass	percussion	woodwinds
3.	flute	oboe	clarinet
4.	French horn	trumpet	trombone
5.	clarinet	saxophone	bassoon
6.	trumpet	trombone	tuba

ASSESSMENT 2: UNIT 2 (CONTINUED)

What You Can Do

Move with Rhythm

Sing "Somebody's Knockin' at Your Door," on page 53, and perform a four-beat body percussion ostinato as you sing.

Sing "*Riqui rán,*" on page 66, while performing small steady-beat movements during the verse.

Play the Notes

Play this recorder part with the recording of "*Riqui rán.*" Play once through silently in chin position and then play aloud.

Move to Show Form

Listen to "River," on page 58, and create a movement for the **A** section and a different movement for the **B** section. Then perform the movements as you sing the song.

© PEARSON EDUCATION, INC.

Name _____   Class _____

Assessment 3: Unit 3

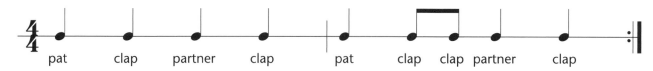

Move to show meter in 4. With a partner, **perform** this body percussion ostinato as you **sing** "Rise and Shine."

4/4 ♩ ♩ ♩ ♩ | ♩ ♫ ♩ ♩ :||

pat   clap   partner   clap   pat   clap clap partner   clap

Identify whether these melodies are in *do-* or *la*-pentatonic. Write your answers directly above each musical example.

1. _____

2. _____

3. _____

4. _____

Compose a melody using the G-pentatonic scale. Choose either *do* or *la* as your tonic.

© PEARSON EDUCATION, INC.

Grade 4, Teacher Edition, pages 99 and 109

B-9

ASSESSMENT 3: UNIT 3 (CONTINUED)

Review, Assess, Perform, Create

What Do You Know?

1. Look at the notation for "Weevily Wheat," on page 105, and answer these questions.

   a. Where is *do* located in the music? _____

   b. What are the letter names for *do*, *re*, *mi*, *so*, and *la* in this song?

      do _____   *re* _____   *mi* _____   *so* _____   *la* _____

   c. Count all the notes that are named *so₁* and *la₁*. Write your answers in the spaces provided.

      so₁ _____   *la₁* _____

2. Perform these examples using rhythm syllables and patting.

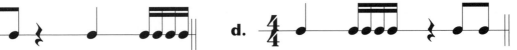

🔘 What Do You Hear? 3   String Instruments

Listen to each excerpt and circle which string instrument is being played.

1.   *koto*   cello

2.   violin   banjo

3.   viola   *sitar*

ASSESSMENT 3: UNIT 3 (CONTINUED)

What You Can Do

Read Melody

Read the notation for "See the Children Playin'," on page 107, and identify whether the song is *do-* or *la-*pentatonic. Sing the song using pitch syllables and hand signs. Sing the song again using the words.

Play Rhythms

Sing "Ōsamu kosamu," on page 96. Perform the ostinato accompaniment on page 97 by patting the rhythms on your thighs. Then sing the song and play the accompaniment on the percussion instruments.

Find Sounds

Perform the speech piece "Bundle-Buggy Boogie Woogie," on page 120. Practice the rhythm ostinatos on page 122 and then perform them with the speech piece. Look around your classroom and home for materials that produce musical sounds when struck by a mallet. Create other ostinatos in 4/4 time and play them using those sounds. Be sure to use the ♫♫ pattern. Perform these patterns with "Bundle-Buggy Boogie Woogie."

ASSESSMENT

ASSESSMENT 4: UNIT 4

Show what you know and **read** the following rhythm patterns.

1. [♩ ♩ ♩♩♩♩ ♩ ‖]   3. [♫ ♩ ♫♩ ♩ ‖]

2. [♫♫ ♫ ♫ ♩ ‖]   4. [♫ ♫ ♫ ♫♩ ‖]

Create four rhythm patterns of your own using . **Notate** your patterns. Add words to match the rhythm. Then have a partner clap them.

1. 𝄴 _____ ‖

2. 𝄴 _____ ‖

3. 𝄴 _____ ‖

4. 𝄴 _____ ‖

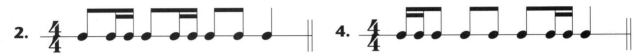

Assessment 4: Unit 4 (continued)

Show What You Know!

These melodies contain all of the notes you have learned. **Sing** each melody. Do any sound familiar?

1. $\frac{3}{4}$

so   so   so   so   fa   mi   fa   fa

2. $\frac{2}{4}$

so   mi   fa   so   mi   fa   so   so   fa   mi   fa   re

3. $\frac{4}{4}$

mi   fa   so   mi   mi   fa   so   mi   mi   fa   so   mi   so   fa   mi

ASSESSMENT

ASSESSMENT 4: UNIT 4 (CONTINUED)

Review, Assess, Perform, Create

What Do You Know?

1. Circle the symbol below for *fortissimo*. What does it mean? Write your answer in the space provided.

pp   p   mp   mf   f   ff _____

2. If you saw the symbol *p*, how would you perform the music?

_____

⊙ What Do You Hear? 4   Rhythm

Circle the correct letter below that matches the rhythms performed on the recording.

1. a.  **b.**

2. a.  **b.**

3. a.  **b.**

© PEARSON EDUCATION, INC.

ASSESSMENT 4: UNIT 4 (CONTINUED)

What You Can Do

Move to Show Contour

Sing "Amazing Grace," on page 160, with eyes closed. Move your hand in an arc to show the contour of the melody.

Play Rhythms

Perform all four of the percussion lines of "*Wu long,*" on page 157, using rhythm syllables. Perform the piece as a group using body percussion. Have different people play each part. Perform the piece again using percussion instruments.

Move to Show Form

Sing "Ode to Joy," on page 152. Perform small, steady-beat movements during the **a** phrases and different movements during the **b** phrase.

Sing with Texture

Sing "America, the Beautiful," on page 158. Create a thick texture by singing the melody and the countermelody together.

ASSESSMENT

ASSESSMENT 5: UNIT 5

Perform these rhythms using rhythm syllables.

Using the rhythms above, **compose** your own rhythm pattern. Make it four measures long. Be sure there are four beats in each measure. **Perform** it for the rest of the class.

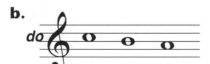

1. Circle the note *ti* in these examples. Then **sing** each example using pitch syllables.

a.   b.   c.

2. Identify the songs or listening selections that have these patterns. Find other songs in the book that use the new note *ti*. Write the song titles below.

_____

_____

_____

_____

Assessment 5: Unit 5 (continued)

Review, Assess, Perform, Create

What Do You Know?

1. Look at the notation for "The Computer," on page 199.

   a. What pitch is named *do* in this song? _____

   b. Point to all the pitches that are called *ti*. How many did you identify? _____

   c. Do the same activity for the pitches named *so*, *fa*, *mi*, *la*, *re*, and *do*.

     so _____   fa _____   mi _____   la _____   re _____   do _____

2. Match each of these tempo words with the correct definition. Write the letters of your answers in the spaces provided.

   a.   *andante*   _____ very fast

   b.   *moderato*   _____ slow

   c.   *allegro*   _____ moderate

   d.   *adagio*   _____ walking speed

   e.   *presto*   _____ fast

ASSESSMENT

Assessment 5: Unit 5 (continued)

What Do You Hear? 5　　Ensembles

Listen to these examples and write a check mark next to the ensemble you hear.

1. ____ brass quintet　　____ classical music trio

____ pop group　　____ Indian classical music ensemble

2. ____ brass quintet　　____ classical music trio

____ pop group　　____ Indian classical music ensemble

3. ____ brass quintet　　____ classical music trio

____ pop group　　____ Indian classical music ensemble

4. ____ brass quintet　　____ classical music trio

____ pop group　　____ Indian classical music ensemble

● ASSESSMENT 5: UNIT 5 (CONTINUED)

What You Can Do

Sing Rounds and Rhythms

Sing "*Los niños en España cantan,*" on page 197, as a round. Create and perform steady-beat movement patterns that reflect the tempo and meter of the song.

Read and Sing *ti*

Sing "Missy-La, Massa-La," on page 188, from the notation using hand signs and pitch syllables. Then sing the song again using the words.

Play Chords

Practice the rhythm patterns for the accompaniment to "Do Wah Diddy Diddy," on page 202. Then sing the song and play the accompaniment on mallet instruments.

Move to Show Form

Perform a rondo speech piece by combining "Heave-Ho," "Going, Going, Gone," and "The Snow," on pages 182–183. Create a different steady-beat movement to accompany each section of the speech piece.

ASSESSMENT

ASSESSMENT 6: UNIT 6

Show What You Know!

Speak "Gotta Find a Footprint" and pay attention to the rhythm of the words. Then **notate** the rhythm of the first two lines of the poem. Next, **perform** the words using your notated rhythms.

_____|

_____‖

Show What You Know!

Here is a melodic sequence, but some of the notes are missing! The first pattern of the melodic sequence is shown. It has only three notes. The sequence continues three more times. Fill in the missing notes. Then **play** the entire sequence on a xylophone or keyboard instrument.

ASSESSMENT 6: UNIT 6 (CONTINUED)

Review, Assess, Perform, Create

What Do You Know?

Match the numbers of the terms below with their definitions. Write your answers in the spaces provided.

1. accent

_____ a melody started at different times

2. theme and variations

_____ a melody pattern repeated at a higher or lower pitch level

3. melodic sequence

_____ stress on certain notes

4. round

_____ a melody repeated with changes

What Do You Hear? 6   Keyboard Timbre

Listen to the following examples of keyboard music. Circle the name of the instrument you hear in each example.

1. piano   harpsichord   organ   synthesizer

2. piano   harpsichord   organ   synthesizer

3. piano   harpsichord   organ   synthesizer

4. piano   harpsichord   organ   synthesizer

ASSESSMENT

Name _____ Class _____

ASSESSMENT 6: UNIT 6 (CONTINUED)

Move to Variations

Listen to *Russian Sailors' Dance,* on page 224, and perform the body percussion pattern. Create your own body percussion part for *Russian Sailors' Dance* and perform it for the class.

Perform with Accents

Sing "*El rancho grande,*" on page 215. Decide where to add accents and then perform them as you sing.

Create with Rhythms

Sing "Dry Bones Come Skipping," on page 218. Perform small steady-beat movements to accompany the **A** sections and different steady-beat movements with the **B** section. Using the rhythms in the song, create a rhythm ostinato. Perform the ostinato on nonpitched percussion instruments as you sing the song.

Move with Sequences

Sing "*Tancovačka,*" on page 230. Perform hand movements to show the contour of the melodic sequences in the verse.

Sing in Rounds

Sing "Let Music Surround You," on page 236, as a round. Always sing with good vocal quality.

© PEARSON EDUCATION, INC.

Book 4, Teacher Edition, page 247

ASSESSMENT: INTRODUCTION

Introduction for the Music Teacher

Checklists

Checklists are provided for performance skills (singing, playing instruments, reading, improvising, moving) and non-performance skills (composing/arranging/notating, listening). Have individual students demonstrate each of the items on the checklists. Guide the students in selecting music and tasks that will permit them to meet all of the goals outlined in the checklists.

You may consider assembling small ensembles in which students with different skill levels all perform a given piece together, but with students playing parts that are appropriate for their various skill levels. When reviewing students' work, continue to refer to the items on the checklists and point out ways their work does or does not meet each of the criteria. For students who do not perform as well as they are capable, provide opportunities to perform small sections of their pieces again. Have the students pay attention to one or two specific points that will improve their work. In this way, assessment becomes an important and contributing part of the learning process.

Rubrics

The rubrics are designed to be used together with the checklists. The goal of performance skills is for all students to perform well, regardless of the difficulty of the material they perform. The goal of non-performance skills is for all students to demonstrate competence, regardless of the difficulty of the composing, arranging, and listening tasks that they are assigned. Of course, some items on the checklists are more important than others, but all of them work together to create successful, expressive music performances, compositions, or informed listening experiences. If you wish to summarize your evaluations of the students' performances or work in a way that allows you to place each student or small group on a graded scale, you may use the rubrics for describing their performances or work.

ASSESSMENT

ASSESSMENT: PERFORMANCE SKILLS

Singing

Checklist for Singing

❑ Posture is upright and relaxed.
❑ Jaw and mouth are relaxed and open.
❑ Breath is inhaled with natural, relaxed expansion of the body.
❑ Tone is free, open, and even throughout range.
❑ Singing is accurate and in tune.
❑ Rhythm is precise and sung with inflection.
❑ Diction is clear (all words are understood).
❑ Volume level is balanced with other members of the ensemble.
❑ Dynamic and rhythmic variations are used to create expressive effects.

Rubric for Singing

❑ **Fluent** The student sings with fluency and ease. There are few errors. All items on the checklist are consistently demonstrated. The performance is confident, beautiful, and expressive.

❑ **Competent** The student sings with relative ease, but several errors or hesitations are present. Most items on the checklist are consistently demonstrated. The performance is confident and expressive.

❑ **More Practice Needed** The student has difficulty performing evenly and in time. Hesitations and errors are clearly evident. Only some of the checklist items are demonstrated. The performance does not convey the expressive intent of the piece performed.

© PEARSON EDUCATION, INC.

Assessment: Performance Skills

Playing Instruments

Checklist for Playing Instruments
❑ Posture is upright and relaxed.
❑ Instruments, sticks, and mallets (when used) are held loosely and comfortably.
❑ Arms, hands, and fingers move easily (no tension evident).
❑ Playing motion is efficient and smooth.
❑ Instrument tone is open, resonant, and even.
❑ Notes are performed accurately and in tune.
❑ Rhythm is accurate and precise.
❑ Tempo is steady and even.
❑ Volume level is balanced with other members of the ensemble.
❑ Dynamic and rhythmic variations are used to create expressive effects.

Rubric for Playing Instruments
❑ **Fluent** The student plays with fluency and ease. There are few errors. All items on the checklist are consistently demonstrated. The performance is confident, beautiful, and expressive.

❑ **Competent** The student plays with relative ease, but several errors or hesitations are present. Most items on the checklist are consistently demonstrated. The performance is confident and expressive.

❑ **More Practice Needed** The student has difficulty performing evenly and in time. Hesitations and errors are clearly evident. Only some of the checklist items are demonstrated. The performance does not convey the expressive intent of the piece performed.

ASSESSMENT

ASSESSMENT: PERFORMANCE SKILLS

Reading

*Checklist for Reading

*❏ Selects appropriate tempo at which to perform unfamiliar music.

*❏ Identifies passages that are not immediately interpretable or technically difficult.

❏ Rehearses difficult or unfamiliar elements in isolation.

❏ Pitches are performed accurately.

❏ Rhythm is accurate and precise.

❏ Rhythm is performed with appropriate inflection.

❏ Style of articulation (if applicable) is accurate and consistent.

❏ Dynamic levels are accurate.

❏ Tempo is steady and even when appropriate.

❏ Rhythmic and dynamic variations are used to create expressive effects.

* Refer to tasks involved in learning unfamiliar music.

Rubric for Reading

❏ Fluent The student reads with fluency and ease. There are few errors. All items on the checklist are consistently demonstrated. The performance is confident, beautiful, and expressive.

❏ Competent The student reads with relative ease, but several errors or hesitations are present. Most items on the checklist are consistently demonstrated. The performance is confident and expressive.

❏ More Practice Needed The student has difficulty performing evenly and in time. Hesitations and errors are clearly evident. Only some of the checklist items are demonstrated. The performance does not convey the expressive intent of the piece performed.

Assessment: Performance Skills

Moving and Improvising

Checklist for Moving
❑ Weight of the body is balanced and secure.
❑ Limbs move easily and without unnecessary tension.
❑ Movements depict the style of music (for example, rhythm, articulation).
❑ Movements are coordinated with the pulse of the music (if applicable).
❑ Changes in movements appropriately mirror changes in the music.
❑ Sizes and distances of movements are appropriate for the occasion and location (for example, on a dance floor, in a circle with classmates, or seated in a chair).

Checklist for Improvising
❑ Notes are grouped in discernible phrases.
❑ Repetition of melodic motives is used to extend and elaborate phrases.
❑ Individual phrases are unified by consistency and continuity.
❑ Phrases are organized with clear, balanced antecedents and consequents.
❑ Harmonic motion (when harmony is present) is logical.
❑ Dynamic and rhythmic variations are used to create expressive effects.
❑ Musical effects are consistent with the improviser's intent.

Rubric for Moving and Improvising
❑ **Fluent** The student moves or improvises with fluency and ease. There are few errors. All items on the checklist are consistently demonstrated. The performance is confident, beautiful, and expressive.

❑ **Competent** The student moves or improvises with relative ease, but several errors or hesitations are present. Most items on the checklist are consistently demonstrated. The performance is confident and expressive.

❑ **More Practice Needed** The student has difficulty performing evenly and in time. Hesitations and errors are clearly evident. Only some of the checklist items are demonstrated. The performance does not convey the expressive intent of the piece performed.

ASSESSMENT

Assessment: Non-Performance Skills

Composing/Arranging/Notating

Checklist for Composing/Arranging/Notating
❑ Instrument timbres and voice parts are combined effectively.
❑ Notes are grouped in phrases.
❑ Repetition of melodic motives is used to extend and elaborate phrases.
❑ Individual phrases are unified by consistency and continuity.
❑ Phrases are organized with clear, balanced antecedents and consequents.
❑ Harmonic motion (when harmony is present) is logical.
❑ Part-writing (if applicable) follows the conventions of the style of composition.
❑ Dynamic and rhythmic variations are used to create expressive effects.
❑ Musical effects are consistent with the intent of the composer or arranger.
❑ Musical sounds are accurately transcribed using formal, informal, or invented notation.
❑ Notation is clear and readable by others.

Rubric for Composing/Arranging/Notating
❑ **Fluent** The composition or arrangement is expressive, beautiful, and consistent with the intent of the composer or arranger. All items on the checklist are consistently demonstrated.

❑ **Competent** The composition or arrangement is well organized and consistent with the intent of the composer or arranger. Most items on the checklist are consistently demonstrated.

❑ **More Practice Needed** The composition or arrangement is somewhat organized and may not be consistent with the intent of the composer or arranger. Only some of the checklist items are demonstrated.

ASSESSMENT: NON-PERFORMANCE SKILLS

Listening

Checklist for Listening

The first four items on this checklist pertain to behavior while listening; the remaining four pertain to auditory discriminations explained after listening.

❑ Remains quiet (when appropriate) while listening to live or recorded music.
❑ Remains stationary (when appropriate) while listening to live or recorded music.
❑ Moves appropriately while listening to music (for example, tapping to the beat, dancing) in social settings where movement is appropriate.
❑ Acknowledges performers with applause (when appropriate).
❑ Describes the timbres of musical tones and labels instruments and voice parts.
❑ Describes the formal organization of sounds (for example, the use of repetition, melodic contour, motivic development).
❑ Describes the emotional effects that the music elicits from self and others.
❑ Describes possible functions of the music in cultural contexts.

Rubric for Listening Discrimination

❑ **Fluent** All aspects of the music are accurately described, and the observations about the music are informative and interesting. All items on the checklist are consistently demonstrated.

❑ **Competent** Most aspects of the music are accurately described, and the observations about the music are informative. Most items on the checklist are consistently demonstrated.

❑ **More Practice Needed** Aspects of the music are described, but some important information is inaccurate or omitted. Only some of the checklist items are demonstrated.

Assessment Answer Key

Unit 1

Show What You Know! (Rhythm)
1. **a.** "Soldier, Soldier"
   b. "Gakavik"

Show What You Know! (Melody)
1. *so-mi-re-do re-do*
2. *so-mi so-mi do-re mi*
3. *do-mi-mi re-re-re-do*

The tonal center (F) can be identified by the key signature: one flat (B♭) = key of F.

What Do You Know?
1. **a.** *do* = F
   b. *so* = C (9)
   c. *mi* = A (9); *re* = G (4);
   la = D (4); *do* = F (3)
2. **a.** ***mf*** medium loud
   b. ***p*** soft
   c. ***mp*** medium soft
   d. < gradually louder
   e. ***f*** loud
   f. > gradually softer

What Do You Hear? 1
Answers will vary and are open to interpretation. Here are some possibilities.
1. smooth, masculine, strong
2. feminine, smooth, clear
3. feminine, lyrical, floating
4. rough, masculine, low

Unit 2

Show What You Know! (Rhythm)
1. Kodály-based rhythm syllables:
   syn-co-pa ti-ti ti-ti ta-a-a-am
   "Somebody's Knockin' at Your Door"

Show What You Know! (Melody)
1. *do re mi-do do do-do do*
2. F G A-F F F-F F
3. *mi-mi re-do mi-so so mi-mi re do*
   B-B A-G B-D D B-B A G

What Do You Know?
1. four
2. **a.** "Hey, m'tswala," "River"
   b. "Hashewie," "Sourwood Mountain,"
   "Riquirrán," "Eh, cumpari!," "Canoe Song"
3. *adagio, andante, moderato, allegro, presto*

What Do You Hear? 2
1. woodwinds
2. brass
3. oboe
4. French horn
5. bassoon
6. tuba

Unit 3

Show What You Know! (Melody)
1. *la*-pentatonic
2. *do*-pentatonic
3. *la*-pentatonic
4. *do*-pentatonic

What Do You Know?
1. **a.** *do* = G
   b. *do* = G, *re* = A, *mi* = B, *so* = D, *la* = E
   c. *so$_l$* = 8, *la$_l$* = 7
2. Kodály-based rhythm syllables:
   a. *ta ti-ti ti-ri-ti-ri ta*
   b. *ti-ri-ti-ri ta-am ta*
   c. *ti-ti [rest] ta ti-ri-ti-ri*
   d. *ta ti-ri-ti-ri [rest] ti-ti*

What Do You Hear? 3
1. *koto*
2. violin
3. *sitar*

ASSESSMENT ANSWER KEY (CONTINUED)

Unit 4

Show What You Know! (Rhythm)

Kodály-based rhythm syllables

1. *ta ta ti-ri-ti-ri ta*

2. *ti-ti-ri ti-ti-ri ti-ti ta*

3. *ti-ti ta ti-ti-ri ta*

4. *ti-ri-ti ti-ti ti-ti-ri ta*

Show What You Know! (Melody)

The first melody is the opening phrase of *"Cantando mentiras."*

What Do You Know?

1. *ff* ; very loud

2. softly

What Do You Hear? 4

1. b

2. a

3. b

Unit 5

Show What You Know! (Rhythm)

Kodály-based rhythm syllables:

1. *tam ti ta ta*

2. *ti tam ta ta*

Show What You Know! (Melody)

1. a. *do-ti-do*

b. *do-ti-la*

c. *la-ti-do*

What Do You Know?

1. a. *do* = C

b. There is one pitch named *ti*.

c. *so* = G (6), *fa* = F (10), *mi* = E (8), *la* = A (1), *re* = D (8), *do* = C (3)

2. a. *andante*   walking speed

b. *moderato*   moderate

c. *allegro*   fast

d. *adagio*   slow

e. *presto*   very fast

What Do You Hear? 5

1. Indian classical music ensemble

2. Pop group

3. Classical music trio

4. Brass quintet

Unit 6

Show What You Know! (Melody)

What Do You Know?

1. accent—stress on certain notes

2. theme and variations—a melody with changes

3. melodic sequence—a melody pattern repeated at a higher or lower pitch level

4. round—a melody started at different times

What Do You Hear? 6

1. organ

2. synthesizer

3. piano

4. harpsichord

Teacher Notes

Graphic Organizers

Table of Contents

GRAPHIC ORGANIZER

Graphic Organizer 1

Comparison

Alike	Different

GRAPHIC ORGANIZER 2

Information Organizer Chart

GRAPHIC ORGANIZER 3

KWHL Chart

What I know	
What I want to know	
How I will learn this	
What I learned	

GRAPHIC ORGANIZER 4

Semantic Feature Analysis

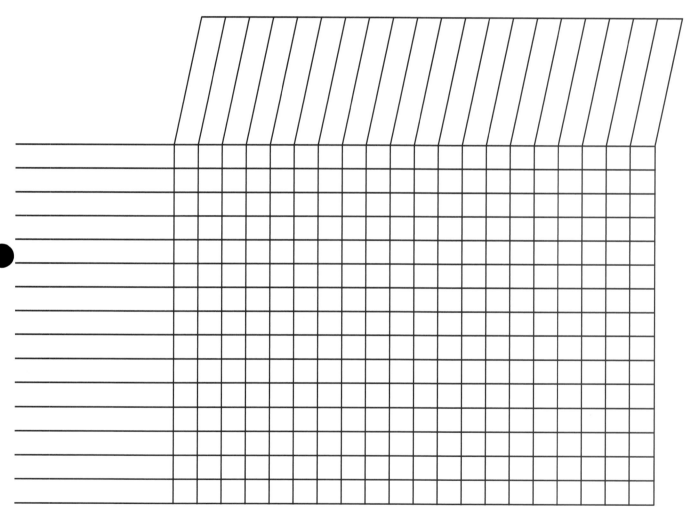

GRAPHIC ORGANIZER 5

Semantic Map

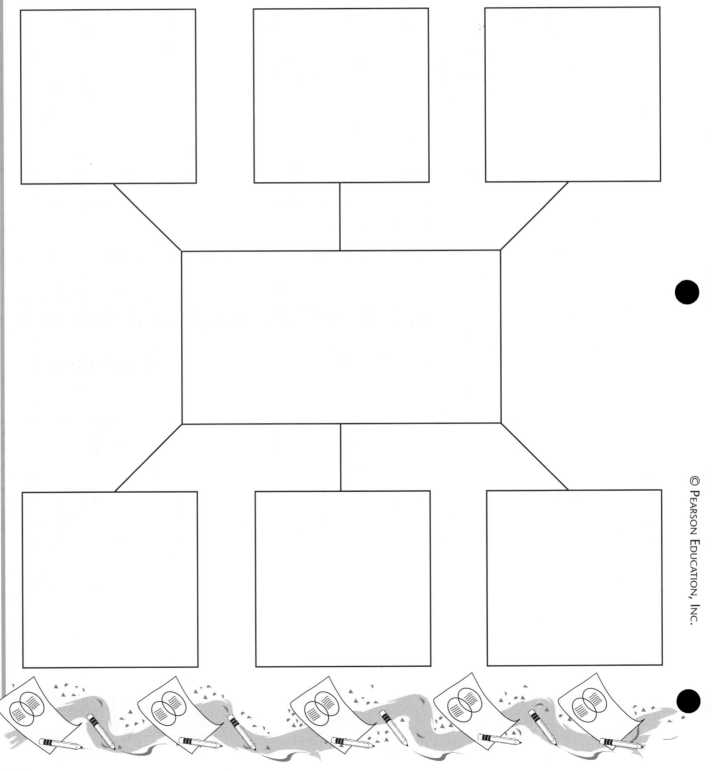

Name _____ Class _____

Story Map

Title: _____

Setting
Characters:
Place:
Time:

▼

Problem:

▼

Events
Leading to
Resolution

→ | |
| --- |
| |

▼

→ | |
| --- |
| |

▼

→ | |
| --- |
| |

▼

→ | |
| --- |
| |

▼

Resolution:

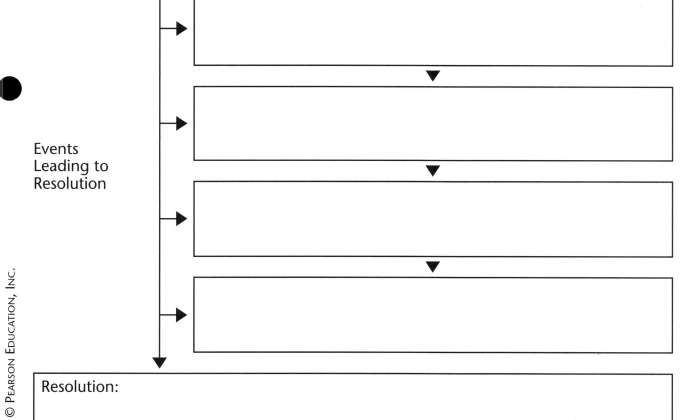

GRAPHIC ORGANIZER 7

Venn Diagram

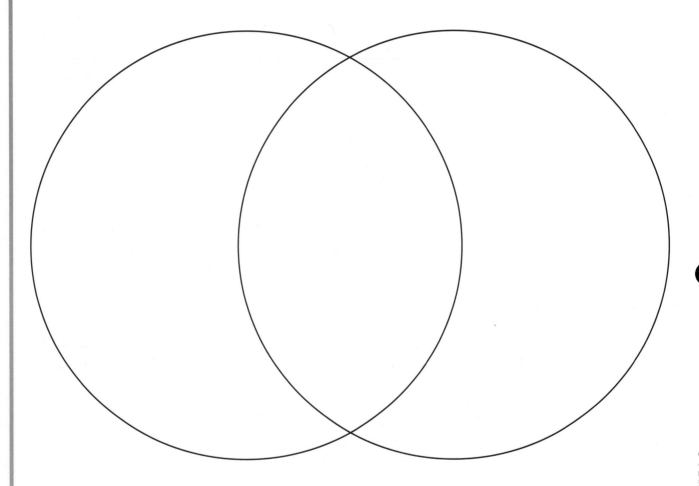

Music Reading Worksheets
Table of Contents

MUSIC READING WORKSHEET 1

Writing Rhythms

Use any combination of the rhythms below to complete these measures. Remember to check the time signature!

1. $\frac{4}{4}$ ___ ♫ ___ 𝄽

2. $\frac{4}{4}$ ♩ ___ ___ ___

3. $\frac{4}{4}$ ___ ___ 𝅗𝅥

4. $\frac{4}{4}$ 𝅗𝅥. ___ ___ ___

Clap and count your measures. Now trade with a friend. Combine your patterns to create eight-measure patterns.

MUSIC READING WORKSHEET 2

Playing Around with the Pentatonic Scale

Create your own pentatonic patterns for the following rhythms. You can sing or play each one as an ostinato, or combine them to make a countermelody. Or, use your new composition as a B-section for an arrangement of *"Tsuki."* You might even want to write new text to go along with your new melody.

do   re   mi   so   la

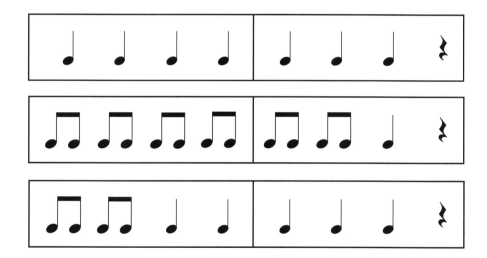

Music Reading Worksheet 2 (continued)

| la |
| so |
| |
| mi |
| re |
| do |

You can read a pentatonic scale from the pitch ladder. Where are the steps in the scale? Where are the skips?

Using hand signs, sing the pentatonic scale going up and then back down again.

You can also read the pentatonic scale from the staff.

The **do** symbol will help you find your way around.

The **do** symbol is found in the first space. That means that any note written in that space is *do.* Find the other notes of the pentatone on the staff. (Hint: Remember to count the lines and spaces from the bottom of the staff.)

© Pearson Education, Inc.

MUSIC READING WORKSHEET 3

Reading Rhythm Patterns

Draw a (circle) around the number of the rhythm pattern that fits the lyrics of "Somebody's Knockin' at Your Door."

Somebody's Knockin' at Your Door

African American Spiritual

1.

2.

3.

4.

MUSIC READING WORKSHEET 4

Find the Hidden ♪♪♪ Patterns

Clap and count these rhythms while singing "Rock Island Line." Write ties in the notation to match the lyrics. Can you find the hidden ♪♪ ♪ patterns? Write them above the tied rhythms.

Railroad Song
New Words and New Arrangement by Huddie Ledbetter
Edited with New Additional Material by Alan Lomax

Rock Island Line

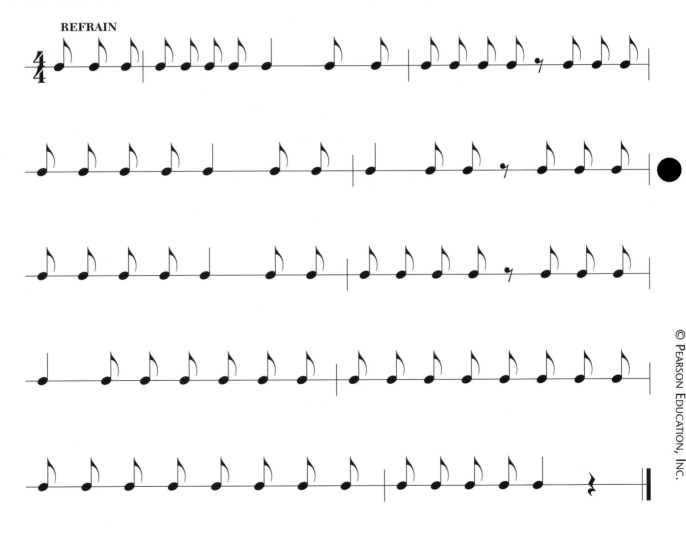

© PEARSON EDUCATION, INC.

MUSIC READING WORKSHEET 4 (CONTINUED)

Once you know the ♪♩♪ pattern, you can count the rhythms below. Clap and say each one, using rhythm syllables.

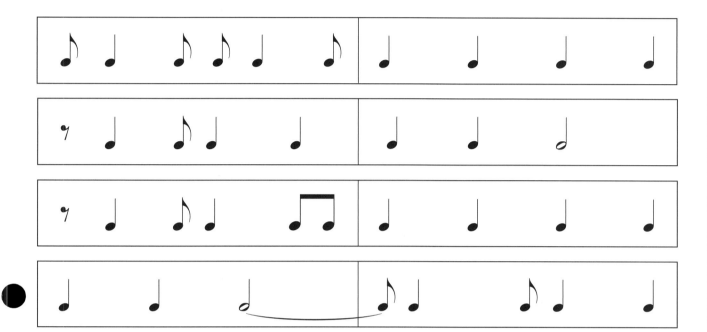

Music Reading Worksheet 5

Recognizing Rhythms

Clap and count the rhythm, then read and sing the notes using hand signs.
Do you recognize the melody?

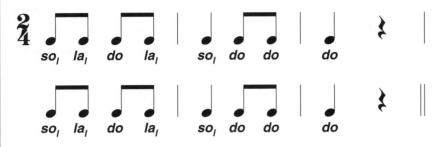

Now notate it on the staff!

MUSIC READING WORKSHEET 6

Reading the Pentatonic Scale

la

so

mi

re

do

la₁

so₁

You can read a pentatonic scale from the pitch ladder. Where are the steps in the scale? Where are the skips?

Using hand signs, sing the pentatonic scale going up and then back down again.

Now find the missing note!

You can also read the extended pentatonic scale from the staff.

The **do** symbol will help you find *do*.

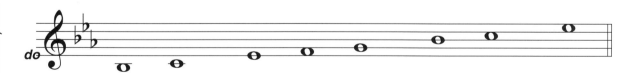

MUSIC READING WORKSHEET 7

Filling in Missing Beats

Sing the lyrics of "Paw-Paw Patch" as you tap a steady beat. Then sing it again as you clap the rhythm. How many *sounds* did you clap on the beats in the blank spaces? (Remember, some words have more than one syllable!)

Paw-Paw Patch

Play-Party Song from the United States

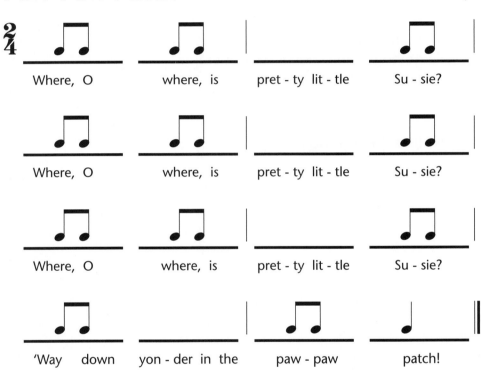

When there are four even sounds on a beat, you can notate them using sixteenth notes.

Fill in the missing beats in "Paw-Paw Patch," above.

© PEARSON EDUCATION, INC.

        Grade 4, Teacher Edition, page 92

MUSIC READING WORKSHEET 7 (CONTINUED)

Fill in the beats below with rhythms that you know. Use 𝄽 at least once in each phrase. Now clap your composition as a counter-rhythm to "Paw-Paw Patch."

$\frac{2}{4}$ _____ | _____ | _____ | _____ |

_____ | _____ | _____ | _____ |

_____ | _____ | _____ | _____ |

_____ | _____ | _____ | _____ ‖

MUSIC READING WORKSHEET 8

Writing the Pentatonic Scale

la
so
mi
re
do
la,
so,

Read the pitches of the extended pentatonic scale from the pitch ladder.

1. Notate these pitches on the staff below, in G-*do*.

2. Now notate them in F-*do*.

3. Notate them one more time, this time in C-*do*.

Name _____ Class _____

MUSIC READING WORKSHEET 9

More Pentatonic Patterns

After warming up with the pitch ladder, read the exercise below in pitch syllables, using hand signs. (G=*do*)

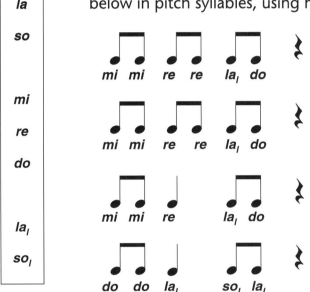

| la |
| so |
| mi |
| re |
| do |
| la, |
| so, |

mi mi re re la, do

mi mi re re la, do

mi mi re la, do

do do la, so, la,

Write the pitch syllables used in the exercise above (from lowest to highest) in the blanks below. Circle the final note. Then notate each note on the staff. The **do** symbol will help you find *do*.

_____ _____ _____ _____ _____

do 𝄞 _____

_____ _____ _____ _____

Now write the letter name of each note (from lowest to highest) in the blanks above.

This exercise uses the _____ - _____ scale. What scale is used in

"See the Children Playin'"? _____

© PEARSON EDUCATION, INC.

MUSIC READING WORKSHEET 9 (CONTINUED)

Notate the pitches of the *la*-pentatonic scale on each staff below. (You will need to use ledger lines for some of the notes.) Use the **do** symbol to figure out where *la₁* should be notated on the staff. Then fill in the blanks with the correct letter names.

1. *do*

   la₁ = _____   *do* = _____

2. *do*

   la₁ = _____   *do* = _____

3. *do*

   la₁ = _____   *do* = _____

Grade 4, Teacher Edition, page 106

MUSIC READING WORKSHEET 10

One Mixed-up Melody!

These patterns are all mixed up! Cut them out and put them in order, and they will make up a song you know. You can sing the pitch syllables, using hand signs . . . just hum the missing note.

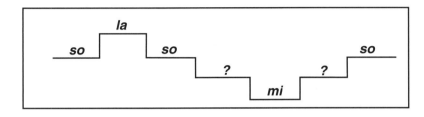

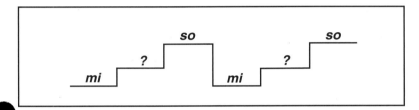

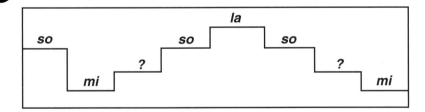

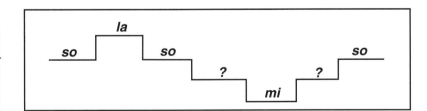

Is there a line missing? Decide where it goes, and what the notes should be.

MUSIC READING WORKSHEET 11

Creating Rhythms

Clap and count these patterns, then fill in the rest of the beats with rhythms that you know. What does each line have in common?

Grade 4, Teacher Edition, page 134

Name _____ Class _____

MUSIC READING WORKSHEET 12

Notating Rhythms

Ala Da'lona

Arabic Folk Song

Learn to notate the rhythm patterns in *"Ala Da'lona"* by tracing the dotted lines below.

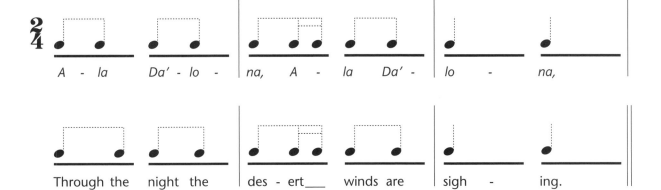

Now notate the rhythm patterns on your own!

MUSIC READING WORKSHEET 13

Name That Rhythm!

Review the rhythms below.

♩	quarter note	one sound on a beat
♫	eighth notes	two even sounds on a beat
𝄽	quarter rest	one silent beat
♬	sixteenth notes	four even sounds on a beat
♪♬	eighth and sixteenth notes	three uneven sounds on a beat (long - short, short)

What is the one thing ALL of the rhythms above have in common? Each rhythm occurs on one beat. Use the rhythms to create your own four-beat patterns.

1. Clap this pattern while you say the last phrase of "Cumberland Gap." Is it the same, or different?

2. Use the tie to make the rhythm fit the words. Write it in the rhythm below.

Way   low   down   in   Cum-ber-land _____   Gap.

3. That's one way to write the rhythm, but there is an easier way to show it, using eighth and sixteenth notes.

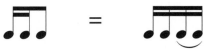

4. Use the rhythms you know to notate the last phrase.

_____   _____   _____   _____

Way   low   down   in   Cum-ber-land _____   Gap.

Music Reading Worksheet 14

Reading the Six-Note Scale

la
so
○
mi
re
do

Using hand signs, sing the pentatonic scale going up and then back down again. Where are the steps in the scale? Where are the skips?

Listen for the new note and write it on the pitch ladder.

You can also read the six-note scale from the staff.
The **do** symbol will help you find do.

do

MUSIC READING WORKSHEET 14 (CONTINUED)

Notate the following motives on the staff in G-*do*.
Don't forget your time signature and bar lines.

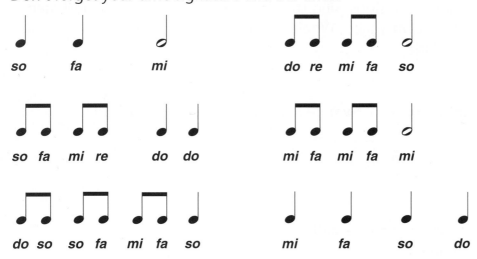

so	fa	mi		do	re	mi	fa	so

so fa mi re | do do   mi fa mi fa mi

do so so fa mi fa so   mi fa so do

do

do

do

MUSIC READING WORKSHEET 15

Finding Half Steps and Whole Steps

Find out about half steps and whole steps with this keyboard.

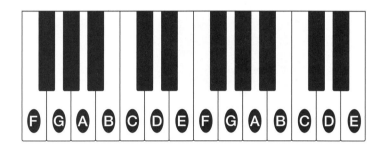

		half step			
do	*re*	*mi*	*fa*	*so*	*la*
G	A	B	C	D	E
C	D	E	F	G	A

What happens when *do* is F? Find the note on the keyboard that will make the pattern of whole and half steps work out. (Hint: Is the correct note a white key, or a black key?)

do	*re*	*mi*	*fa*	*so*	*la*
F	G	A	?	C	D

Fill in the names of the notes below. Notice the key signature!

pitch syllables: _____ _____ _____ _____ _____ _____

letter names: _____ _____ _____ _____ _____ _____

MUSIC READING WORKSHEET 16

Tied Up in Notes

Clap this pattern as you say the words. Is the pattern the same or different?

La Tarara

Folk Song from Spain

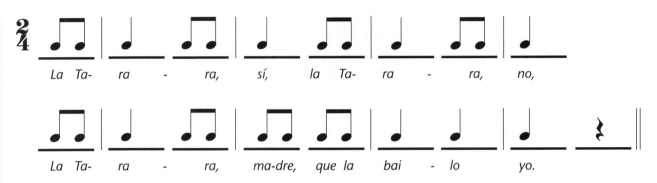

La Ta- ra - ra,   sí,   la Ta- ra - ra,   no,

La Ta- ra - ra,   ma-dre, que la bai - lo   yo.

Use the tie to transform the rhythm above into the rhythm of the words. Where will you draw the tie?

That's one way to write the rhythm, but there is another, easier way.

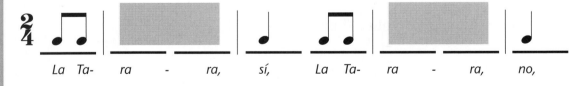

Use the new rhythm to complete the phrase.

La Ta- ra - ra,   sí,   La Ta- ra - ra,   no,

La Ta- ra - ra,   ma-dre, que la bai - lo   yo.

MUSIC READING WORKSHEET 17

Recognizing Rhythm Patterns

Clap this pattern as you say the words. Is the pattern the same or different?

Old House, Tear It Down!

*African American Folk Song
Collected by John Work*

Old   house,   tear it _____ down!

Use the tie to transform the rhythm above into the rhythm of the words.
Where will you draw the tie?

That's one way to write the rhythm, but there is another, easier way.

Notate the new rhythm to complete the phrase.

Old   house,   tear it _____ down!

READING WORKSHEETS

MUSIC READING WORKSHEET 18

Name That Tune!

Write in the pitch syllables in the blanks below, then sing the song with hand signs.
(Your teacher will sing the missing note.) Describe the missing note. Is it higher or lower
than *la*? Is it higher or lower than *do¹*?

Name the song: _____

MUSIC READING WORKSHEET 19

A New Note

Read and sing this tune, using pitch syllables and hand signs.
Then notate it on the staff below.

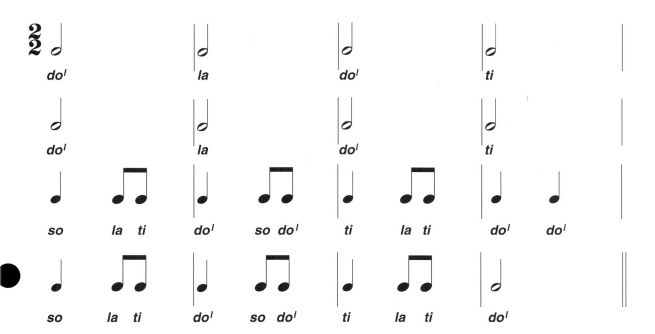

You can sing this tune as a countermelody to "Missy-La, Massa-La." Make up your own
lyrics, or sing the pitch syllables. Play it on an instrument.

Music Reading Worksheet 20

Triple Meter Tricks

Draw the bar lines in the correct place in this mystery song, then clap and count it.
You can take turns conducting meter in 3.

Music Reading Worksheet 21

Harmony: The Coloring of Music

Circle the notes of the I chord in red.

Circle the notes of the IV chord in blue.

Circle the notes of the V_7 chord in green.

do	**re**	**mi**	**fa**	**so**	**la**	**ti**	**do**^{I}	**re**^{I}	**mi**^{I}	**fa**^{I}	**so**^{I}
I			IV	V_7							

MUSIC READING WORKSHEET 22

Curwen Hand Signs

  do¹

  ti

  la

  so

  fa

  mi

  re

  do

MUSIC READING PRACTICE
Table of Contents

Recordings of the Reading Sequence exercises in this section are provided in the CD package.

READING PRACTICE

MUSIC READING PRACTICE: SEQUENCE 1

Rhythm: Reading ♪♩, ♩, and ♩

Use rhythm syllables to **read** and **perform** this two-part rhythm accompaniment.

Soldier, Soldier

*Traditional Song from the
United States and England*

MUSIC READING PRACTICE: SEQUENCE 2

Rhythm: Reading ♫ and ♩ in Duple Meter

Use rhythm syllables to **read** and **perform** this rhythm accompaniment.

Gakavik (The Partridge)

Folk Song from Armenia

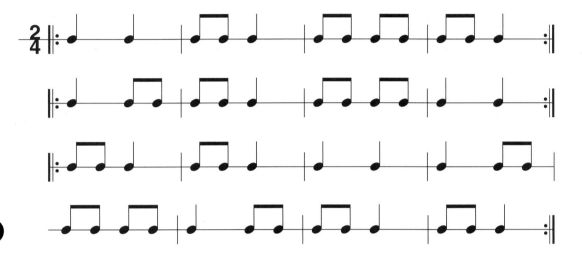

READING PRACTICE

MUSIC READING PRACTICE: SEQUENCE 3

Melody: Reading Steps, Skips, Repeated Pitches

For inner-hearing practice, **read** and **sing** this countermelody.
Use pitch syllables and hand signs.

Gonna Ride Up in the Chariot

African American Spiritual

MUSIC READING PRACTICE: SEQUENCE 4

Melody: Reading Pentatonic Patterns

Use pitch syllables and hand signs to **read** and **sing** this countermelody.

Tsuki (The Moon)

School Song from Japan

READING PRACTICE

MUSIC READING PRACTICE: SEQUENCE 5

Rhythm: Reading with Ties

Use rhythm syllables to **read** and **perform** this two-part rhythm accompaniment.

Somebody's Knockin' at Your Door

African American Spiritual

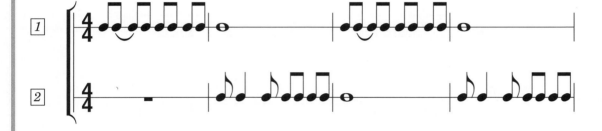

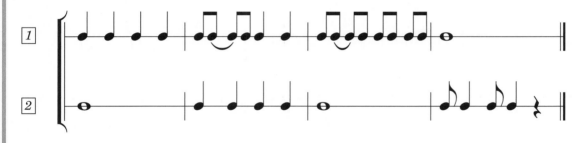

Music Reading Practice: Sequence 6

Rhythm: Reading ♪ ♩ ♪

Use rhythm syllables to **read** and **perform** this rhythm accompaniment.

Railroad Song
New Words and New Arrangement
by Huddie Ledbetter
Edited with New Additional Material by Alan Lomax

Rock Island Line

"Rock Island Line" New words and music arrangement by Huddie Ledbetter. Edited with new additional material by Alan Lomax.
TRO - © Copyright 1959 (Renewed) Folkways Music Publishers, Inc., New York, New York. Used by permission.

MUSIC READING PRACTICE: SEQUENCE 7

Melody: Reading *la,* and *so,*

Use pitch syllables and hand signs to **read** and **sing** this melody accompaniment.

Hashewie (Going 'Round)

Folk Song from Eritrea, Africa

MUSIC READING PRACTICE: SEQUENCE 8

Melody: Reading *do¹*

For inner-hearing practice, **read** and **sing** this countermelody.
Use pitch syllables and hand signs.

Sourwood Mountain

Folk Song from the Appalachian Mountains

mi   so so la   so so do¹   so   mi re do

do   do do la₁   do   mi   so   mi so do

do   do do la₁   do   mi so so la   mi re do

READING PRACTICE

MUSIC READING PRACTICE: SEQUENCE 9

Rhythm: Reading ♫ , ♩. , ♬♬

Use rhythm syllables to **read** and **perform** this two-part rhythm accompaniment.

Paw-Paw Patch

Play-Party Song from the United States

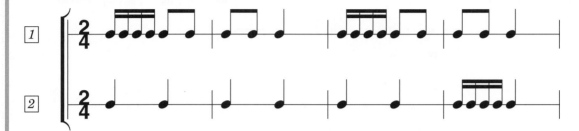

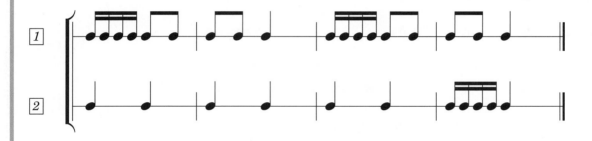

MUSIC READING PRACTICE: SEQUENCE 10

Rhythm: Reading ♩, 𝄽, ♫, ♪♩ ♪ in Meter in 4

Use rhythm syllables to **read** and **perform** this counter-rhythm.

Rise and Shine

Folk Song from the United States

READING PRACTICE

MUSIC READING PRACTICE: SEQUENCE 11

Melody: Reading *la₁* and *so₁*

Read and **sing** both written versions of this melody accompaniment.
Use pitch syllables and hand signs.

Weevily Wheat

Traditional

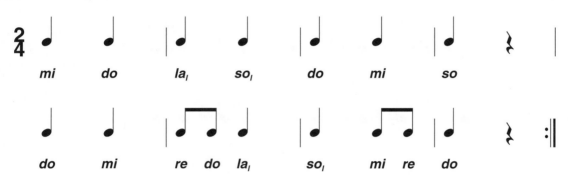

mi do la₁ so₁ do mi so

do mi re do la₁ so₁ mi re do

MUSIC READING PRACTICE: SEQUENCE 12

Melody: Reading *la*-Pentatonic Patterns

Use pitch syllables and hand signs to **read** and **sing** this countermelody.

See the Children Playin'

MUSIC READING PRACTICE: SEQUENCE 13

Rhythm: Reading Upbeats

Use rhythm syllables to **read** and **perform** this rhythm accompaniment.

Ochimbo

Folk Song from Kenya

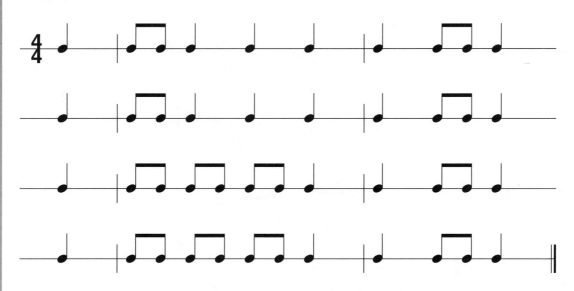

MUSIC READING PRACTICE: SEQUENCE 14

Rhythm: Reading ♪♫♫, ♫♫

Use rhythm syllables to **read** and **perform** this rhythm accompaniment.

Cumberland Gap

Play-Party Song from Kentucky

READING PRACTICE

MUSIC READING PRACTICE: SEQUENCE 15

Melody: Reading *do*, *re*, *mi*, *fa*, *so*

Use pitch syllables and hand signs to **read** and **sing** this melody accompaniment.

Canción de cuna (Cradle Song)

Folk Song from Latin America

MUSIC READING PRACTICE: SEQUENCE 16

Melody: Reading *fa* in a New Key

Use pitch syllables and hand signs to **read** and **sing** this countermelody.

Chairs to Mend

Street Call from England

READING PRACTICE

MUSIC READING PRACTICE: SEQUENCE 17

Rhythm: Reading 𝅘𝅥𝅭 and ♪

Use rhythm syllables to **read** and **perform** this rhythm accompaniment.

La Tarara

Folk Song from Spain

Music Reading Practice: Sequence 18

Rhythm: Reading ♪ and ♩.

Use rhythm syllables to **read** and **perform** this rhythm accompaniment.

Old House, Tear It Down!

African American Folk Song
Collected by John Work

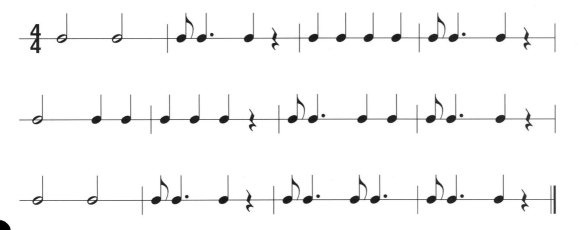

READING PRACTICE

MUSIC READING PRACTICE: SEQUENCE 19

Melody: Reading *ti*

Read and **sing** both written versions of this countermelody. Use pitch syllables and hand signs.

Kookaburra

Words and Music by Marion Sinclair

so   la   fa   so   do¹   mi   fa   re   mi   so

so   la   ti   do¹   so   fa   mi   so   la   ti   do¹

do

MUSIC READING PRACTICE: SEQUENCE 20

Melody: Reading *ti* and the Major Scale

Use pitch syllables and hand signs to **read** and **sing** this melody accompaniment.

Missy-La, Massa-La

Game Song from the Caribbean

Name _____   Class _____

Rhythm: Reading in Meter in 3

Use rhythm syllables to **read** and **perform** this counter-rhythm.

Oh, How Lovely Is the Evening

Traditional German Melody

© PEARSON EDUCATION, INC.

● MUSIC READING PRACTICE: SEQUENCE 22

Rhythm: Reading in Meter in 4

Use rhythm syllables to **read** and **perform** this counter-rhythm.

Dry Bones Come Skipping

Traditional Song from the United States

READING PRACTICE

MUSIC READING PRACTICE: SEQUENCE 23

Melody: Reading a Melodic Sequence

Use pitch syllables and hand signs to **read** and **sing** this melody accompaniment.

Thula, thula, ngoana (Sleep, Sleep, Baby)

Folk Song from the Lesotho Region of South Africa

MUSIC READING PRACTICE: SEQUENCE 24

Melody: Reading a Melodic Sequence

Use pitch syllables and hand signs to **read** and **sing** this melody accompaniment.

Tancovačka (Dancing)

Slovak Folk Song

READING PRACTICE

E-25

Teacher Notes

ORFF

Table of Contents

ORFF

ORFF 1

*Traditional Song from England
and the United States
Arranged by Konnie Saliba*

Soldier, Soldier

For abbreviations of instruments, see Instrumentarium on page F-36

ORFF 2

Somebody's Knockin' at Your Door

African American Spiritual
Arranged by Konnie Saliba

ORFF

ORFF 3

Rock Island Line

Railroad Song
New Words and New Arrangement by Huddie Ledbetter
Edited with New Additional Material by Alan Lomax

© PEARSON EDUCATION, INC.

●Orff 3 (continued)

Orff 3 (CONTINUED)

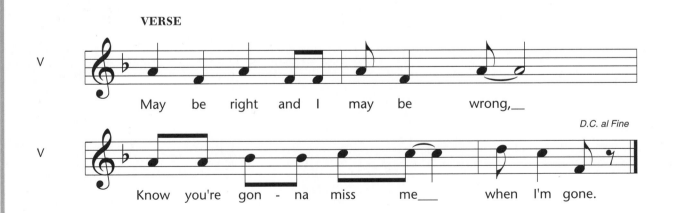

Grade 4, Teacher Edition, page 54

●Orff 4

Paw-Paw Patch

Play-Party Song from the United States

ORFF 5

Weevily Wheat

Traditional
Arranged by Konnie Saliba

*Add SG-AG at measure 9.

● ORFF 6

Divide SX-AX part between two players.

- One student plays E and G.
- One student plays A and B.

Words by Reginald Royal
Folk Melody from Mississippi
Arranged by Konnie Saliba

See the Children Playin'

ORFF

ORFF 7

Canción de cuna (Cradle Song)

Folk Song from Latin America
Arranged by Konnie Saliba

(play any 2 notes)

ORFF 8

All Night, All Day

African American Spiritual
Arranged by Konnie Saliba

ORFF

Kookaburra

Words and Music by Marion Sinclair
Arranged by Konnie Saliba

●Orff 9 (continued)

SG-AG

AX

AM

TeB

Gu

●BX-CBX

Orff

ORFF 10

Game Song from the Caribbean
Collected and Documented by Allan Lomax, J.D. Elder and Besse Lomax Hawes
Arranged by Konnie Saliba

Missy-La, Massa-La

*The CBX part may be played on guitar.

© PEARSON EDUCATION, INC.

Grade 4, Teacher Edition, page 188

ORFF 10 (CONTINUED)

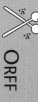

Orff 11

Dry Bones Come Skipping

Traditional Song from the United States
Arranged by Konnie Saliba

Grade 4, Teacher Edition, page 218

Name _____   Class _____

● ORFF 12

Beriozka (The Birch Tree)

Folk Song from Russia
Arranged by Konnie Saliba

*Add SG and AG on repeat.

ORFF 13

The Bard of Armagh

Folk Tune from Ireland
Arranged by Konnie Saliba

Orff 13 (continued)

ORFF 14

Tina singu

Folk Song from Lesotho, Africa
Arranged by Konnie Saliba

ORFF 15

Sakura

Folk Song from Japan
Arranged by Konnie Saliba

*Use wooden mallets or stick end of regular mallets on SM, AM, and BM.

ORFF

ORFF 16

Feng yang hua gu (Feng Yang Song)

Folk Song from China
Arranged by Konnie Saliba

*Use wooden mallets or stick end of regular mallets on SM, AM, and BM.

ORFF **17**

Yibane amenu

Round from Israel
Arranged by Konnie Saliba

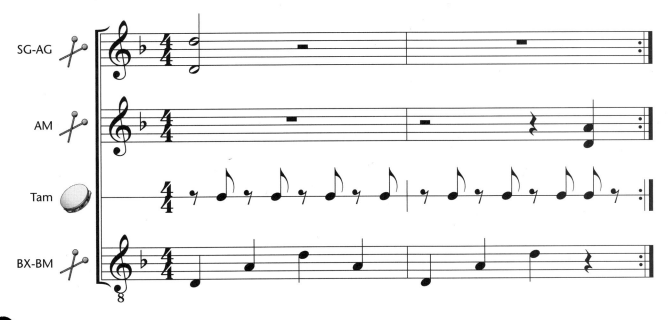

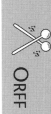

ORFF

ORFF 18

Wings of a Dove

Folk Song from the West Indies
Arranged by Konnie Saliba

*CBX part may be doubled on guitar.

Grade 4, Teacher Edition, page 318

● ORFF 18 (CONTINUED)

ORFF 18 (CONTINUED)

● O**RFF** 19

Clementine

Folk Song from the United States
Arranged by Konnie Saliba

O**RFF**

Grade 4, Teacher Edition, page 341

F-27

Orff 19 (continued)

Name _____   Class _____

Orff **20**

Peace Round

Traditional
Arranged by Konnie Saliba

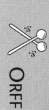

ORFF

ORFF 21

Cindy

Folk Song from the Southern United States
Arranged by Konnie Saliba

Grade 4, Teacher Edition, page 384

ORFF 21 (CONTINUED)

ORFF

Grade 4, Teacher Edition, page 384

Orff **22**

Al quebrar la piñata (Piñata Song)

Christmas Song from Mexico
Arranged by Konnie Saliba

ORFF 22 (CONTINUED)

Orff 23

Dayenu (It Would Have Been Enough)

Jewish Passover Song
Arranged by Konnie Saliba

ORFF 23 (CONTINUED)

Stop on fermata last time.

SG-AG

AX

Cb

Tam

CD

BX-CBX

ORFF

ORFF 24

INSTRUMENTARIUM

Abbreviations of Instruments on a Score

Winds

SoR	Sopranino Recorder
SR	Soprano Recorder
AR	Alto Recorder
TR	Tenor Recorder
BR	Bass Recorder

Mallet Instruments

SG	Soprano Glockenspiel
AG	Alto Glockenspiel
SX	Soprano Xylophone
AX	Alto Xylophone
BX	Bass Xylophone
CBX	Contrabass Xylophone
SM	Soprano Metallophone
AM	Alto Metallophone
BM	Bass Metallophone

Percussion—Metals

Tr	Triangle
FC	Finger Cymbals
JB	Jingle Bells
CT	Chime Tree
AB	Agogo Bells
CB	Cow Bell
Cym	Cymbals
W	Slide Whistle

Percussion—Woods

WB	Wood Block
ToB	Tone Block
C	Castanets

Sh	Shakers
M	Maracas
Cb	Cabasa
R	Ratchet
Rt	Rattles
TeB	Temple Blocks
VS	Vibra Slap
Cl	Claves
Gu	Guiro
LD	Log Drum
SB	Sand Blocks
Af	Afuchi

Percussion—Membranes or Skins

HD	Hand Drum
Tam	Tambourine
BD	Bongo Drums
CD	Conga Drum
SD	Snare Drum

Large Percussion

HC	Hanging Cymbal
G	Gong
BD	Bass Drum

Tuned Instruments

G	Guitar
P	Piano
Tp	Timpani
DB	Double Bass

Orff 25

Instrumentarium Diagram

Bongos

Temple Blocks

Kettle Drums

Small percussion on table

Bass Xylophone

Alto Xylophones

Soprano Xylophones

Bass Metallophone

Alto Metallophones

Soprano Metallophones

Bass Xylophone

Soprano Glockenspiels

Alto Glockenspiels

Orff

Teacher Notes

SIGNING

Table of Contents

SIGNING 1

Put a Little Love in Your Heart

*Words and Music by Jimmy Holiday,
Randy Myers, and Jackie De Shannon*

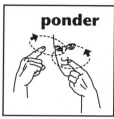
ponder

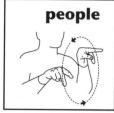
people

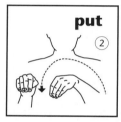
help ①

Think of your fellow man,   lend him a helping hand,

put ②

love

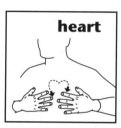
in

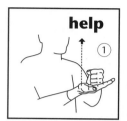
heart

Put a   little love   in your   heart.

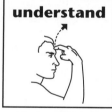
understand

time

late

please

You see, it's   getting   late,   oh, please

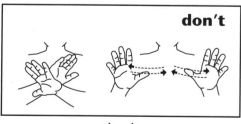
don't

wait

don't   hesitate,

① move from chest out

② direct sign to heart

SIGNING 1 (CONTINUED)

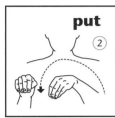
put ②
Put a

love
little love

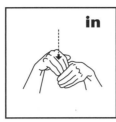
in
in your

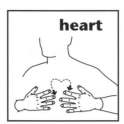
heart
heart.

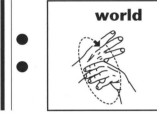
world
And the world

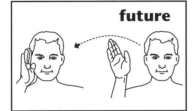
future
will be a

better
better place,

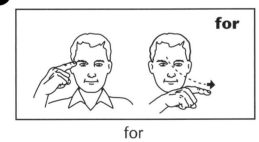
for
for

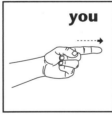
you
you

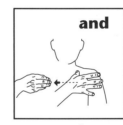
and
and

me
me.

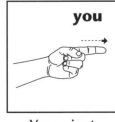
you
You just

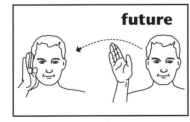
future
wait

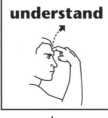
understand
and see.

② direct sign to heart

In American Sign Language (ASL), some signs have a different meaning depending on their direction. In this song, "I'll help you…" is signed by having the sign "help" move from the body out. If another person is helping the signer, the sign moves in to the signer.

SIGNING 2

The Lion Sleeps Tonight

Words and Revised Music by George David Weiss,
Hugo Peretti, and Luigi Creatore

VERSE 1

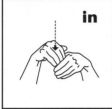
in

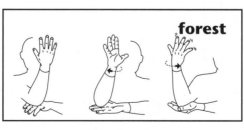
forest

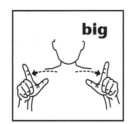
big

In the | jungle, the | mighty

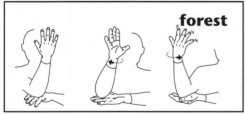
forest

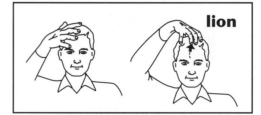
lion

sleep

jungle, the | lion | sleeps

tonight

tonight.

in

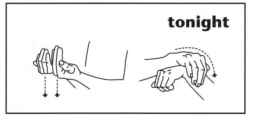
forest

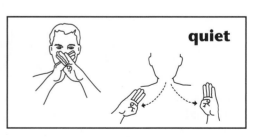
quiet

In the | jungle, the | quiet

SIGNING **2** (CONTINUED)

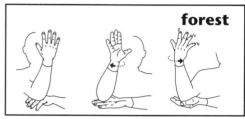
forest

jungle, the

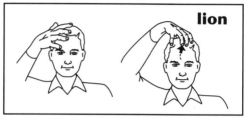
lion

lion

sleep

sleeps

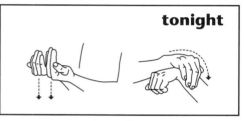
tonight

tonight.

VERSE 2

near

Near the

village

village, the

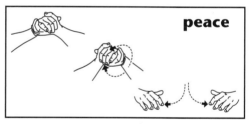
peace

peaceful

village

village, the

lion

lion

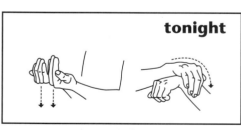
sleep

sleeps

tonight

tonight.

Signing 2 (continued)

near

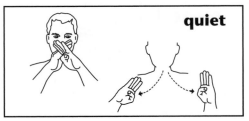

village

quiet

village

Near the	village, the	quiet	village, the

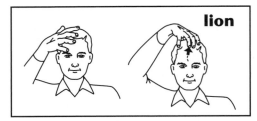

lion

sleep

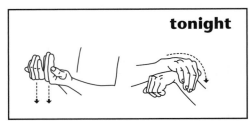

tonight

lion	sleeps	tonight.

SIGNING 2 (CONTINUED)

VERSE 3

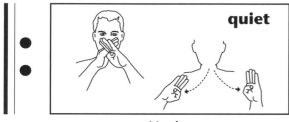

① palm flat
against chest

Hush,   my   darling,

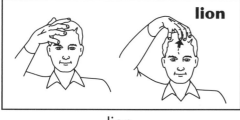

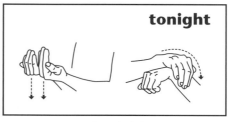

don't fear, my   darling, the

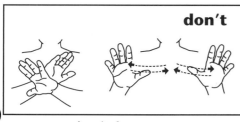

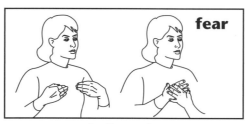

lion   sleeps   tonight.

The sign for "jungle" is many trees. The sign for "lion" comes from the lion's mane.

SIGNING 3

All Night, All Day

African American Spiritual

REFRAIN

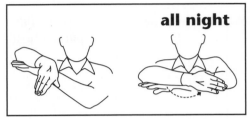
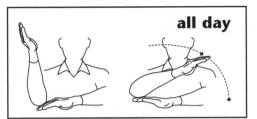

All night,   all day,

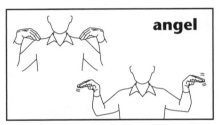

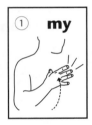
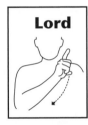

Angels   watching over   me,   my   Lord.

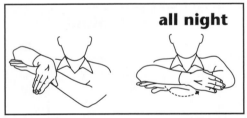
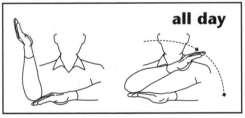

All night,   all day,

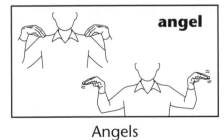

Angels   watching over   me.

① palm flat against chest

Name _____ Class _____

SIGNING

SIGNING 3 (CONTINUED)

VERSE 1

 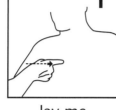 

Now I   lay me   down to sleep,

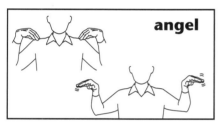 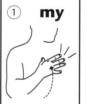 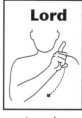 my Lord

Angels   watching over   me,   my   Lord.

  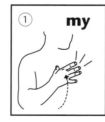 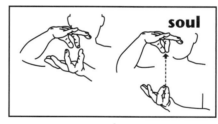 

Pray the   Lord   my   soul to   keep,

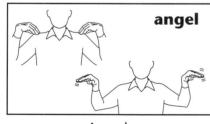  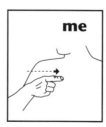

Angels   watching over   me.   *(repeat refrain)*

① palm flat against chest

© PEARSON EDUCATION, INC.

Grade 4, Teacher Edition, page 180   G-9

Signing 3 (continued)

VERSE 2

If

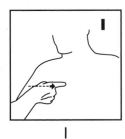

I

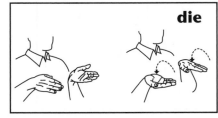

die

before

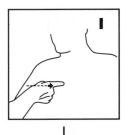

I

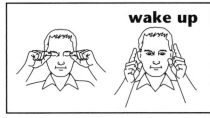

wake,

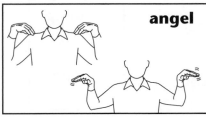

Angels

watching over

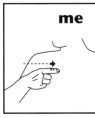

me,

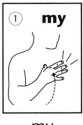

my

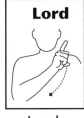

Lord.

Pray the

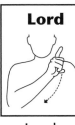

Lord

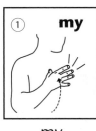

my

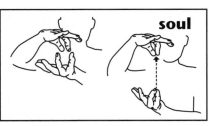

soul to

take,

① palm flat against chest

Signing 3 (continued)

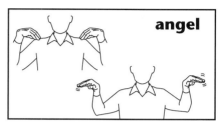  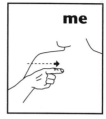

Angels   watching over   me. *(repeat refrain)*

SIGNING 4

Thula, thula, ngoana
(Sleep, Sleep, Baby)

Folk Song from the Lesotho Region of South Africa

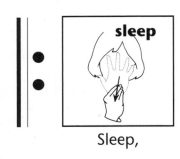
Sleep,

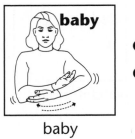
my

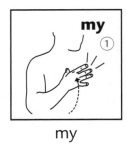
baby

3 times

① palm flat against chest

SIGNING 5

California, Here I Come

*Words and Music by Al Jolson,
Bud Desylva, and Joseph Meyer*

California

California,

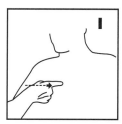

I

here I

go

come.

place

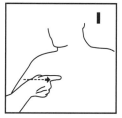

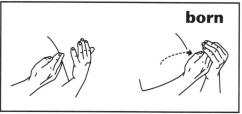
I

born

Right back   where I   started from.

California

Where bowers

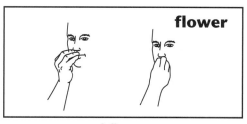
flower

of flowers

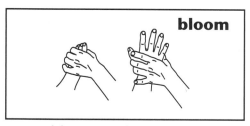
bloom

bloom in the spring.

every morning

Each morning at dawning

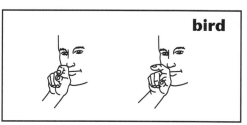
bird

birdies sing and

sing

everything.

Signing 5 (continued)

tan

A sun-kissed

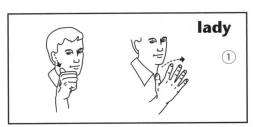
lady ①

miss

say

said,

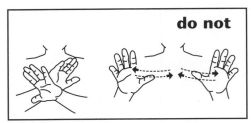
do not

"Don't be

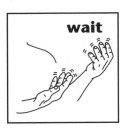
late

late."

reason

That's why

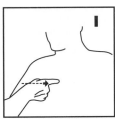
I

I

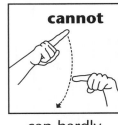
cannot

can hardly

wait

wait.

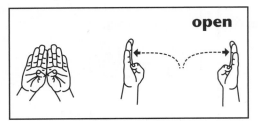
open

Open up that

gold

Golden

bridge

Gate.

① thumb touches chest

● SIGNING 5 (CONTINUED)

 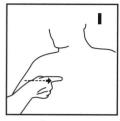 

California,   here I   come!

SIGNING 6

La raspa

Folk Song from Mexico
English Words by Kim Williams

Mexico

dance

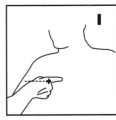
I

dance

The *raspa* | | I will | dance,

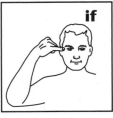
(step forward and back)

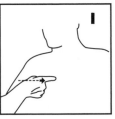
I

dance

as forward and back | I | go.

if

you

want

dance

So if | you | want to | dance,

start

your

(tap heel and then toe)

begin with | your | heel and toe.

SIGNING 6 (CONTINUED)

 **always**

 **move**

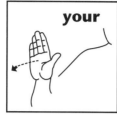 **your**

 **feet**

Always   moving, moving   your   feet,

(step side-close, then jump on the beat)

back and forth, now jump to the beat.

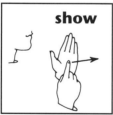 **show**

 **dance**

This is how   the dance we will do,

 **laugh**

 **smile**

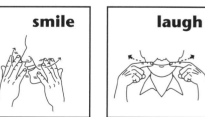 **laugh**

laughing,   laughing all the way through.

SIGNING 6 (CONTINUED)

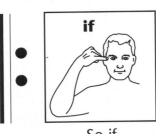
if

So if

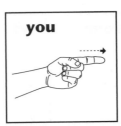
you

you

want

want to

dance

dance

Mexico

the *raspa*

dance

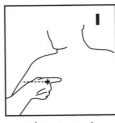
I

the way I

dance

do,

start

Begin

move

to move

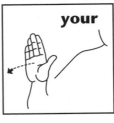
your

your

feet

feet,

you

and you

dance

will be dancing,

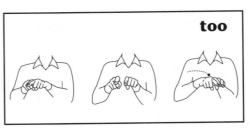
too

too.

SIGNING 7

We Shall Overcome

Freedom Song from the United States

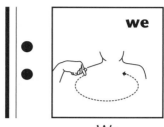
we

We

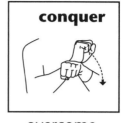
shall

shall

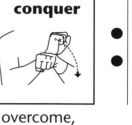
conquer

overcome,

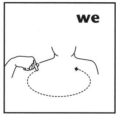
we

We

shall

shall

conquer

overcome

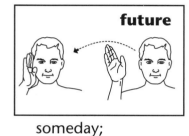
future

someday;

(large movement)

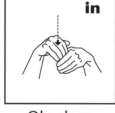
in

Oh, deep

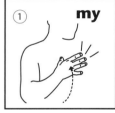
① **my**

in my

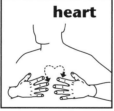
heart

heart

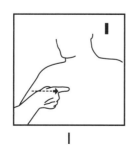
I

I

true

do

believe

believe,

① palm flat against chest

SIGNING 7 (CONTINUED)

**we**	**shall**	**conquer**	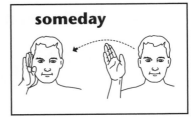**someday** (large, slow movement)
We	shall	overcome	someday.

The words "shall" or "will" are future tense words; therefore, the sign for "shall" or "will" is the same as "someday" (in the future). If the sign is made using a large, slow movement, and with tension, it represents far in the future.

The second verse can be signed with the class holding hands and walking forward to represent the lyrics *We'll walk hand in hand.* The rest of the lyrics for verse 2 should be signed.

© PEARSON EDUCATION, INC.

Name _____ Class _____

● SIGNING **8**

Ocho kandelikas (Eight Little Candles)

Words and Music by Flory Jagoda

VERSE 1

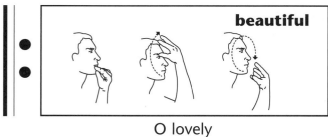
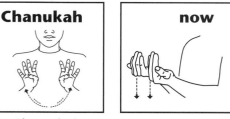

O lovely   Chanukah   is here,

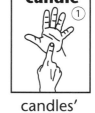
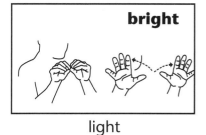

eight   candles'   light   to bring me   cheer.

REFRAIN

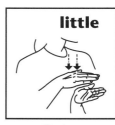
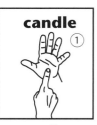

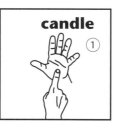

O one   little   candle,   two   little   candles,

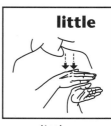

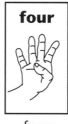
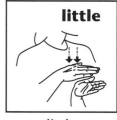
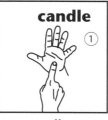

three   little   candles,   four   little   candles,

① fingers wiggle

Signing 8 (continued)

five 	**little** 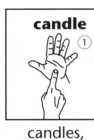	**candle** ① 	**six** 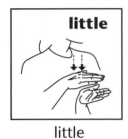	**little** 	**candle** ①
five	little	candles,	six	little	candles,

seven 	**little** 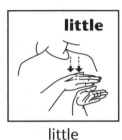	**candle** ① 	**eight** 	**little** 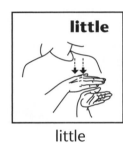	**candle** ① 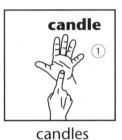
seven	little	candles,	eight	little	candles

all 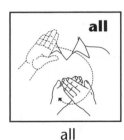	**for** 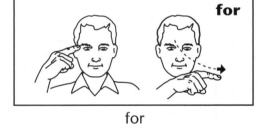	**me** 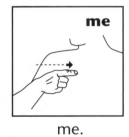
all	for	me.

① fingers wiggle

The sign for "Chanukah" represents the eight candles of the menorah.

The sign for "little" varies depending on the object it is describing. The sign for "little" in this song could also be made with the index finger and thumb, depending on the size of the menorah's candles. What would the sign be for a little child? (Flat hand held out, indicating the height of the child.)

© Pearson Education, Inc.

Manual Alphabet

A   B   C   D   E   F   G

H   I   J   K   L   M   N

O   P   Q   R   S   T   U

V   W   X   Y   Z

SIGNING 10

Numbers

1

2

3

4

5

6

7

8

9

10

Note: Often signed with palm in for numbers 1–5 and palm out for numbers 6–9

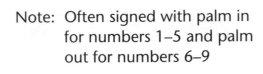

KEYBOARD

Table of Contents

KEYBOARD

© PEARSON EDUCATION, INC.

Keyboard 1

One-Line, Two-Line, Three-Line Reading

Use the black-key locators to determine the placement of the steps and skips on the keyboard.

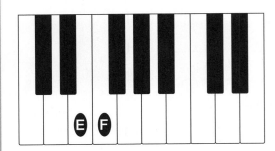

Step Up

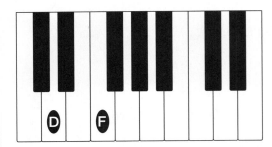

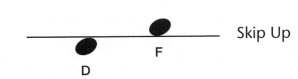

Skip Up

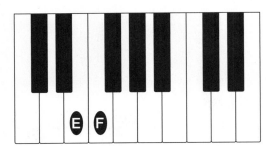

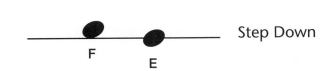

Step Down

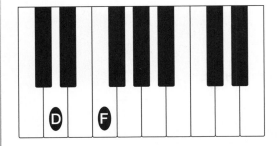

Skip Down

KEYBOARD 1 (CONTINUED)

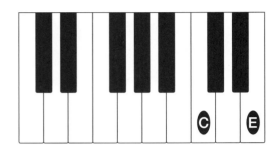

Skip Up

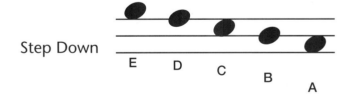

C   E

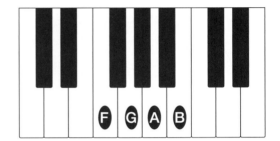

F G A B

Step Up

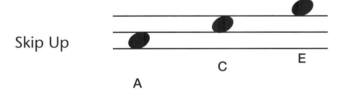

F   G   A   B

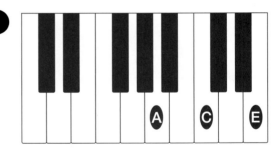

A   C   E

Skip Up

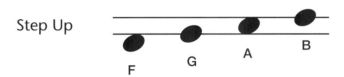

A   C   E

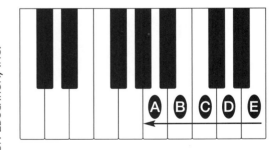

A B C D E

Step Down

E   D   C   B   A

KEYBOARD

KEYBOARD 2

Fingering One-, Two-, Three-Line

Write the finger numbers in the boxes above the notes.

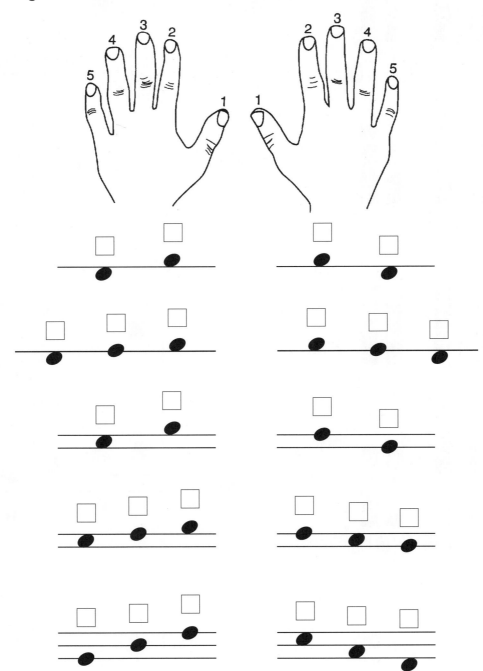

KEYBOARD 3

Five-Line Reading and Fingering

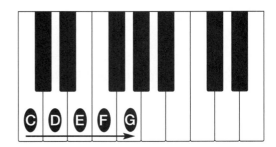

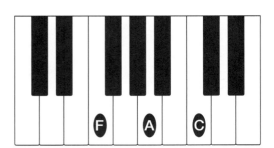

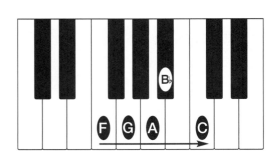

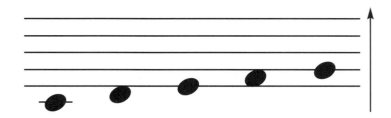

"Up" on the keyboard is to the right.
"Up" on the staff is bottom to top.

Skip Up

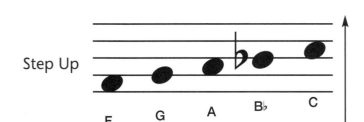

F   A   C

Step Up

F   G   A   B♭   C

Write the finger numbers in the boxes
above the notes.

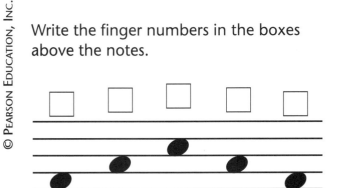

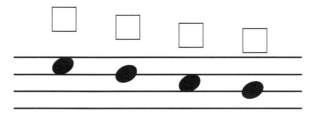

KEYBOARD

KEYBOARD 4

Same and Different

Play the chorus parts. Notice that there are three different patterns. Use the suggested right-hand fingering.

Limbo Like Me

Words and Music Adapted by
Massie Patterson and Sammy Heyward

shift
hand
position
up

KEYBOARD 5

Rhythm Pattern and Triads

Play each chord using left-hand fingers 5, 3, 1.

I'm Gonna Sing

African American Spiritual

A Chord

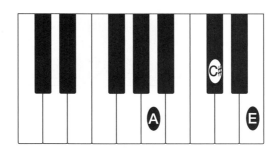

E Chord

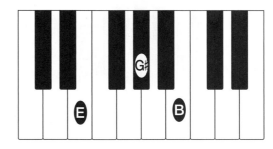

For an easier shift down and up, use your thumb and fifth finger to "guide" the way.

Play the A chord. While holding on to the A with your 5th finger, slide your thumb to the B next door and release. Fingers 5 and 3 are now free to play E and G♯ below.

Now, while holding on to the B with your thumb, slide your 5th finger to the A next door and release. Fingers 3 and 1 are now free to play C♯ and E above.

Practice *sliding* with your eyes closed!

l.h.   1   1
          3   1   3
          5   3   5
                  5

KEYBOARD 6

Walking Bass and Tritone Duet Accompaniment

Play Part 1 or Part 2 of the accompaniment for "Joe Turner Blues."

Joe Turner Blues

Blues Song from the United States

Part 1

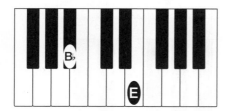

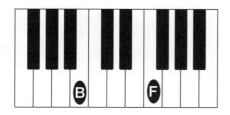

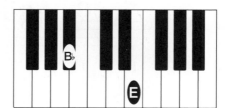

KEYBOARD 6 (CONTINUED)

Part 2

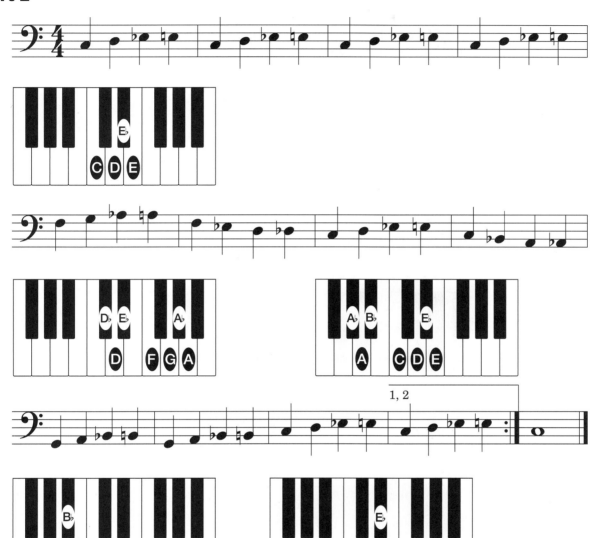

KEYBOARD 7

Playing a Pentatonic Ostinato

Play this ostinato with "Weevily Wheat," using the right hand. Remember to play the pitches *at least* one octave higher than written.

Weevily Wheat

Traditional

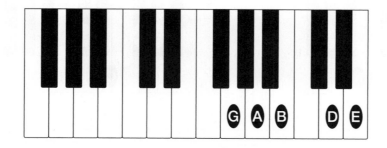

KEYBOARD 8

Playing a Broken-Chord Accompaniment

Practice playing the following three broken-chord shapes using LH 5-1 and RH 1-3 fingerings.

Over My Head

African American Spiritual

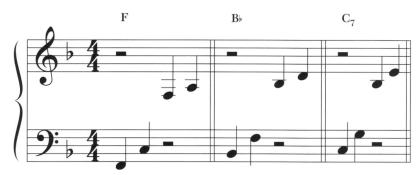

When these patterns are familiar, play the following broken-chord accompaniment. Notice the last measure!

KEYBOARD

KEYBOARD 9

Playing an Accompaniment that Expands the Range

The left-hand accompaniment for "Ala Da'lona" uses three different positions. Notice in the musical example that these positions go beyond the range of five consecutive fingers. To accommodate the expanded range, simply shift the 2nd and 1st left-hand fingers up to A and C. In the "B₇ Position," your hand will return to the original range.

Ala Da'lona

Arabic Folk Song

Em Position

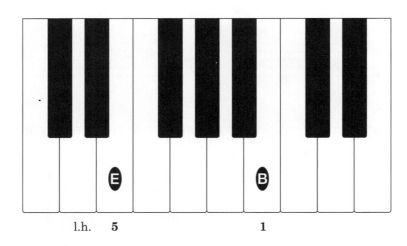

Am Position

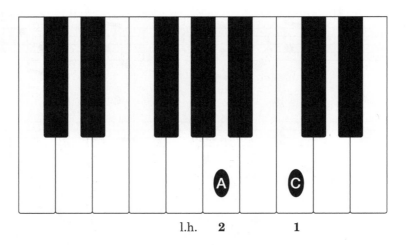

© PEARSON EDUCATION, INC.

Grade 4, Teacher Edition, page 136

KEYBOARD 9 (CONTINUED)

B₇ Position

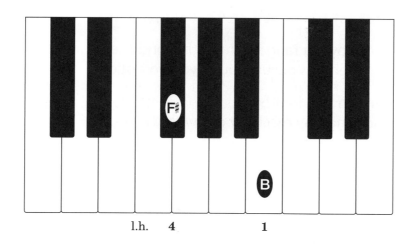

l.h.   4   1

Use this rhythm throughout.

In the measures where there are two positions (Em and Am), use this rhythm.

KEYBOARD 10

Playing a Melody with a Large Stretch

Many times a melody will cover a range of notes beyond the five that fit comfortably under your five fingers. When this occurs you have two options.

1) Split the melody between two hands.
2) Extend the right-hand range by reaching out with the thumb.

Use the second option to play "Ode to Joy."

Ode to Joy

Music by Ludwig van Beethoven

Listen carefully as your teacher plays the melody. Are there phrases that are similar? Are there phrases that are exactly the same? Discuss these.

Measures 12 and 13 contain the "reach down" to the thumb and then the "reach up" to the 3rd finger. Practice several times until the "reaches" are comfortable.

Play the phrases that are similar (1 and 2 or 1 and 4). Say pitch names as you play.

Play the phrases that are exactly the same (2 and 4). Say pitch names as you play.

Play the entire melody. Say pitch names as you play.

Grade 4, Teacher Edition, page 152

KEYBOARD 11

Playing an Accompaniment with ♩.♪

The melody of "La Tarara" uses the rhythm of dotted quarter followed by an eighth note. Notice the use of the same rhythm in the accompaniment. When does the rhythm pattern change? Why does it have to change? What fingering would be appropriate?

La Tarara

Folk Song from Spain

INTRODUCTION

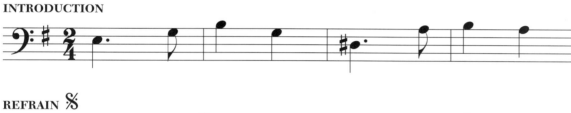

REFRAIN 𝄋

Fine

VERSE

D.S. al Fine

KEYBOARD 12

Using a Thumb Crossing to Play a Melodic Phrase

There are times when the arrangement of black keys and white keys to be played call for an alternate type of fingering. The melodic phrase *Singin' Do wah diddy diddy down diddy do* is such a time. The phrase uses both C♯ and F♯—to begin on the thumb and then use the right-hand finger 4 on F♯ would be awkward.

Practice the following exercise before playing the melodic phrase.

Do Wah Diddy Diddy

Words and Music by Jeff Barry and Ellie Greenwich

When this exercise feels comfortable, try the melodic phrase below.

KEYBOARD 13

Playing a Two-Handed Accompaniment

The chords used in this accompaniment are in closest position. Practice the right-hand chords several times before playing the accompaniment.

Right-Hand Practice Pattern

Create other rhythms appropriate for this verse accompaniment.

Sweet Betsy from Pike

Folk Song from the United States

H-17

KEYBOARD 14

Accompaniment on the Offbeats

Challenge: Play "closest-position" chords on the offbeats.

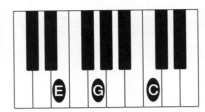 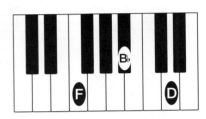 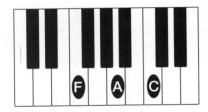

Oh, Susanna

Words and Music by Stephen Foster

Grade 4, Teacher Edition, page 264

KEYBOARD 15

Ensemble Accompaniment

Challenge: Play Parts 2 and 3 together as one part.

Streets of Laredo

Cowboy Song from the United States

Grade 4, Teacher Edition, page 272

KEYBOARD 16

Broken-Chord Accompaniment

Sakura   *Folk Song from Japan*

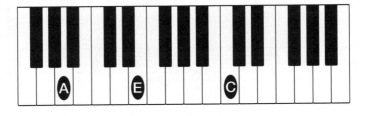

Here are the two broken chords used in the accompaniment above. Practice playing them in rhythm before accompanying the song.

H-20   Grade 4, Teacher Edition, page 308

KEYBOARD 17

Playing a Refrain That Expands the Normal Hand Range

Notice the range (lowest pitch to the highest pitch) of the refrain to "My Bonnie Lies Over the Ocean." The lowest pitch is F and the highest pitch is D. This is beyond the range of five fingers, so fingering adjustments or expansions will need to be used.

Expand the normal range of your hand by moving "away from the thumb." Practice the first example below several times until it is comfortable.

My Bonnie Lies Over the Ocean

Folk Song from the United States

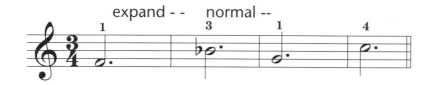

What finger should you begin with on line 2 and line 4 of the refrain?

extend down to 1 for the F on the 3rd line

Practice lines 2 and 4 of the refrain until they are comfortable.

Play the refrain.

KEYBOARD

Playing a Two-Handed Accompaniment

In Unit 4, Lesson 12, you learned about the I and V_7 harmonies. "Clementine" uses these harmonies. Practice the two positions shown below. Notice the rhythm—there is always a rest on the third beat of the measure! Use right-hand fingers 1 and 3 for the G Chord shape. What right-hand fingers would you use for the D_7 Chord shape? If you answered 2 and 3 you are correct!

Experiment with left-hand fingering to determine which is most comfortable for your hand—suggestions might be left-hand finger 2 for the G Chord shape and left-hand finger 3 for the D_7 Chord shape.

Clementine

Folk Song from the United States

G Chord shape

D_7 Chord shape

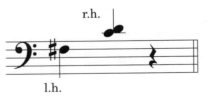

When you feel comfortable with these chord shapes, practice playing the accompaniment. Notice that the pattern is the same for the verse and refrain.

Grade 4, Teacher Edition, page 341

● KEYBOARD 19

Fingering Shifts

For the Beauty of the Earth

Arranged by Conrad Kocher

Phrase 1

Phrase 2

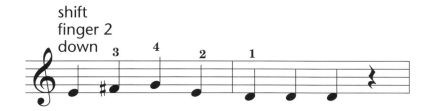

Phrase 3 (same as 1)

Phrase 4 (same as 2)

Phrase 5

Phrase 6

KEYBOARD 20

Expanding the Five-Finger Range

Play the following melodies in the octave shown.

Words and Music by
John Forster and Tom Chapin

The Wheel of the Water

Voice 1   *As written*

Voice 4

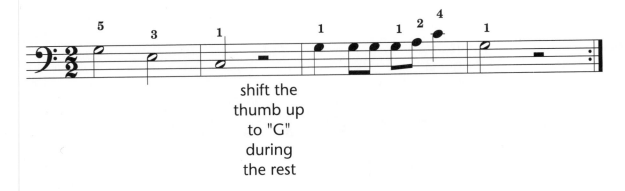

shift the
thumb up
to "G"
during
the rest

Voice 5

Grade 4, Teacher Edition, page 362

●KEYBOARD 21

Playing an Ensemble Accompaniment

Look at the verses for "Little David, Play on Your Harp," on page 394 in your book.
Sing the verses and choose different combinations of the parts below to perform with
each refrain.

Little David, Play on Your Harp

African American Spiritual

KEYBOARD

Grade 4, Teacher Edition, page 394

H-25

Keyboard 21 (CONTINUED)

VERSE

D.C. al Fine

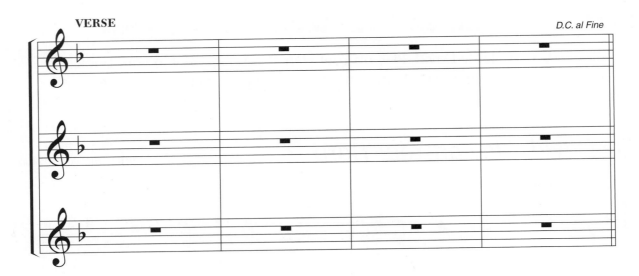

Grade 4, Teacher Edition, page 394

KEYBOARD 22

Using a Rhythm Pattern in Melodic Improvisation

♪ ♩ ♪ is a very common Latin rhythm. Use this rhythm to improvise on the pitches shown below. Some improvisation "examples" have been provided.

Sambalele

Folk Song from Brazil

Example 1

Example 2

KEYBOARD **23**

Playing a Two-Handed Accompaniment

Practice the right-hand closest position chords. Which pitches change and which pitches stay the same? Now practice the alternating-hand accompaniment. When the meter changes, how will you need to change the rhythm of the accompaniment?

Practice Chart

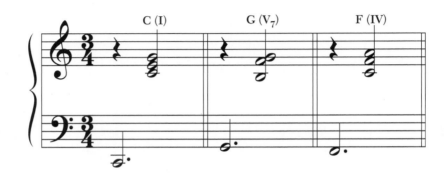

Al quebrar la piñata (Piñata Song)

Christmas Song from Mexico

© PEARSON EDUCATION, INC.

Grade 4, Teacher Edition, page 432

Keyboard 23 (continued)

KEYBOARD

Keyboard 24

Keyboard Template

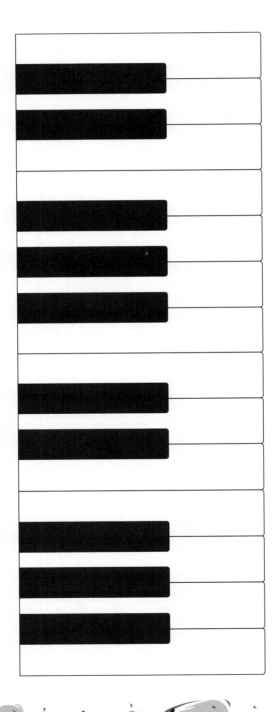

RECORDER

Table of Contents

RECORDER

RECORDER 1

Playing G and A

This recorder part will give you additional practice playing G and A. Decide if you want to play the *Solo* or *Chorus* part. Remember to observe the repeat signs.

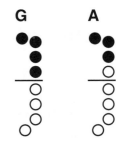

Limbo Like Me

Words and Music Adapted by Massie Patterson and Sammy Heyward

RECORDER 2

Making Choices

If you need additional practice playing G and A, play Countermelody 1. When you are ready to learn new notes, play Countermelody 2 during the refrain of the song.

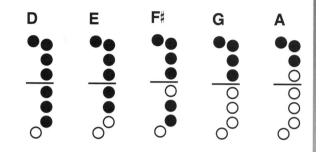

Gonna Ride Up in the Chariot

African American Spiritual

Countermelody 1

VERSE

REFRAIN

Countermelody 2

REFRAIN

RECORDER

RECORDER 3

Recorder Ostinatos

After you have played some of the ostinatos found in your book on p. 36, play the same rhythm patterns on your recorder. Remember to say *daah* on each note in the style of the music.

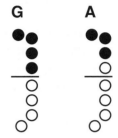

Tie Me Kangaroo Down, Sport

Words and Music by Rolf and Bruce Harris

RECORDER 4

Syncopated Recorder

Before practicing the part below, play this rhythm ♪ ♩ ♪ on your recorder using the note A and the note G. Play this recorder countermelody with the recording of the song. Relate the syncopated measures with the words *Rock Island* during the refrain.

Rock Island Line

Railroad Song

"Rock Island Line" New words and music arrangement by Huddie Ledbetter. Edited with new additional material by Alan Lomax.
TRO - © Copyright 1959 (Renewed) Folkways Music Publishers, Inc., New York, New York. Used by permission.

RECORDER

RECORDER 5

Four-Beat Patterns on "BAG"

Look at the countermelody for "Joe Turner Blues." Notice that it uses mostly G and A. Play this countermelody on your recorder. Play each phrase on one breath, remembering to whisper *daah* on each note. Each phrase ends with a quarter rest.

G   A   B

Joe Turner Blues

Blues Song from the United States

Recorder 6

Feeling Meter in 3

Look at the recorder part below. Notice that most of the time there is a rest on the first beat of each measure. Clap the rhythm of this recorder piece. Clap the "air" on each rest. Now play the recorder part below. When measures begin with a rest, feel the first beat and play on the second and third beats.

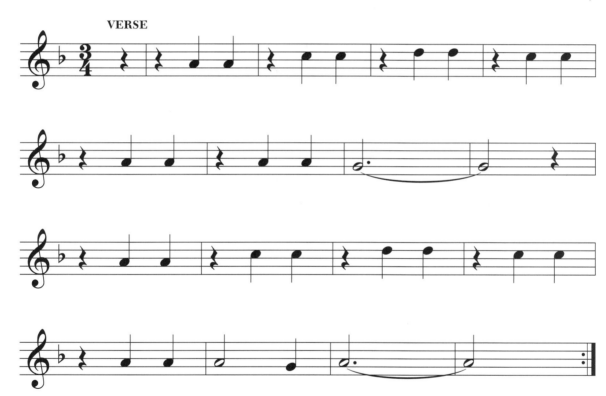

River

Words and Music by Bill Staines

I-7

RECORDER 7

Reading a Melody

As you play this countermelody to accompany *"Riqui rán,"* listen to where the recorder melody is the same as the melody that is being sung. Do not play during the instrumental interludes.

E G A B C

Riqui rán

Folk Song from Latin America

VERSE 1

VERSES 2 and 3

RECORDER 8

Playing in Harmony

Play the parts below with a friend. In order to play in harmony, one of you should read the top staff of each pair while the other reads the bottom staff. Notice that the recorder melody is similar to the traditional Japanese folk melody.

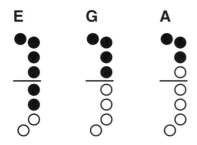

Ōsamu kosamu (Biting Wind)

Folk Song from Japan

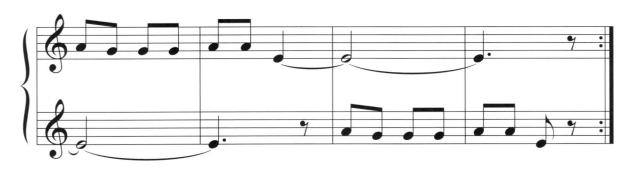

RECORDER

RECORDER 9

Making Choices

Look at the two parts below. One uses G and A while the other uses D, E, G, and A. Choose which part you would like to play. If you choose the second part, remember to whisper *daah* gently on the low notes.

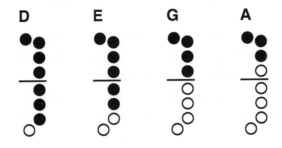

D E G A

Rise and Shine

Folk Song from the United States

Part 1

Part 2

Grade 4, Teacher Edition, page 98

RECORDER 10

Feeling the Steady Beat

As you play this recorder part, feel the beats grouped in sets of 2. Remember to break the sound between notes of the same pitch. Observe that the recorder part has four phrases. Are any of the phrases the same? different?

E   F#   A   B

Weevily Wheat

Traditional

RECORDER

RECORDER 11

Notes in the High Register

Play this countermelody in the style of the music while others sing this popular song. When playing high D, remember to move your thumb only slightly away from the thumb hole.

The Lion Sleeps Tonight

Words and Revised Music by George David Weiss, Hugo Peretti, and Luigi Creatore

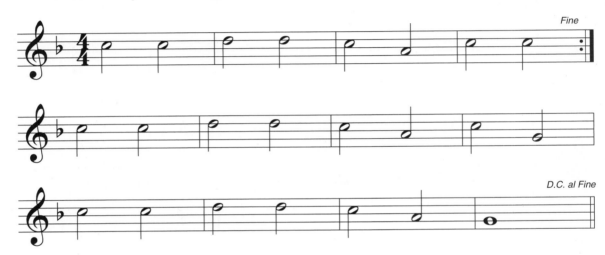

Grade 4, Teacher Edition, page 131

RECORDER 12

Playing with Style

Whisper *daah* in the style of the music as you play this countermelody to accompany the singing of this famous song.

Over the Rainbow

Words by E. Y. Harburg
Music by Harold Allen

RECORDER 13

Playing in Harmony

Play this harmony part on your recorder while a friend plays the traditional melody of "Ode to Joy" found in your student book on page 152. Listen to each other and blend your sound as you play.

D   E   F♯   G   A   B

Ode to Joy

Music by Ludwig van Beethoven

RECORDER 14

Playing with Style

While fingering the notes on your recorder, sing the countermelody below while singing the letter names of the notes. Remember to hold each note for its full value. Then play the same way, feeling the style of the music.

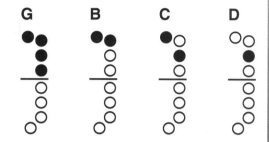

All Night, All Day

African American Spiritual

Fine

D.C. al Fine

RECORDER

Making Choices

Practice the two countermelodies below. Make sure you carefully observe the repeat signs. Which one is more difficult for you to play? Choose the countermelody you would like to play while others sing this song.

D E G A B C

Missy-La, Massa-La

Game Song from the Caribbean

Countermelody 1

Countermelody 2

RECORDER 16

More Choices

Look at the two countermelodies below. Which one will help you practice playing notes in the high register? the low register? Practice both of these countermelodies before choosing the one you would like to play while others sing this song.

D   F#   G   A   B   C   D

Frog Music

Folk Song from Canada

Countermelody 1

Countermelody 2

© PEARSON EDUCATION, INC.

RECORDER

RECORDER 17

Observing Breath Marks

Review the fingering for D, E, F♯, G, and A before playing this countermelody. When playing notes in the low register, remember to use very little air. As you practice this countermelody, play each phrase on one breath (').

D E F♯ G A

The Keel Row

Folk Song from Northumbria

© PEARSON EDUCATION, INC.

● **RECORDER** 18

Feeling Meter in 3

Sing the countermelody below before playing it on your recorder. Make sure you hold the dotted half notes for three full beats. Play the countermelody the same way you sang it. Feel the long phrases as you play.

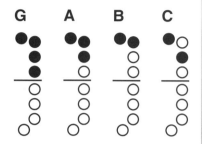

Sweet Betsy from Pike

Folk Song from the United States

RECORDER

RECORDER 19

Playing Notes in the High Register

As you practice this recorder part, remember to whisper *daah* in the style of the music. When playing with others, blend your sound by making sure you can hear the other recorders as you play.

G   A   C   D

Blow, Ye Winds

Folk Song from the United States

VERSE

REFRAIN

Grade 4, Teacher Edition, page 255

RECORDER 20

Working Together

This recorder countermelody has solo and chorus parts like the song. Play the countermelody with a friend. Decide who will play the solo parts and who will play the chorus parts. Another time try switching parts.

D	E	F♯	G	A	B

Shanty from the United States

Rio Grande

RECORDER

RECORDER 21

Notes in the Low Register

D   E   F#   G

Play this countermelody in the style of the music while others sing this folk song. When playing notes in the low register, remember to blow gently to produce a musical sound.

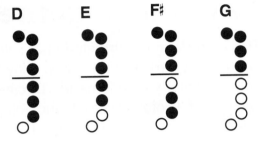

How Can I Keep from Singing?

Celtic Folk Song

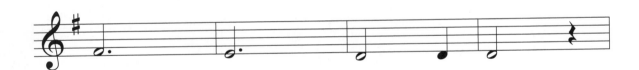

Grade 4, Teacher Edition, page 261

RECORDER 22

Accompanying a Dance

While others sing and dance, play this part on your recorder to accompany *"La raspa."* Feel the beat as you play. Carefully observe all the repeat signs and the rests.

F♯   G   A   B   C

La raspa

Folk Song from Mexico

INTERLUDE

RECORDER

RECORDER 23

Adding More Harmony

Play this countermelody to accompany
"Bogando a la luz del sol."

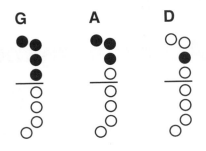

Bogando a la luz del sol
(Rowing Toward the Sunlight)

Folk Song from Venezuela

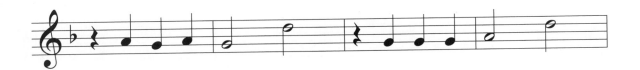

Grade 4, Teacher Edition, page 306

● **RECORDER 24**

Playing Melodic Sequences

Before playing this countermelody, compare the measures in the third line. Notice that the melodic shape is the same, but each measure begins on a lower pitch. This is called a melodic sequence. Practice the third line before playing the entire piece.

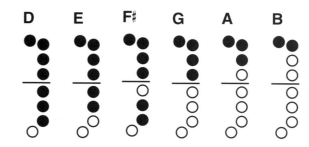

Wings of a Dove

Folk Song from the West Indies

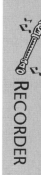

RECORDER

Name _____   Class _____

RECORDER 25

Accompanying an Entire Song

You can play the countermelody below while others sing this famous hobo song. Read the song using rhythm syllables before playing the recorder. Just like the traditional song, the refrain has a different melody from the verse.

Big Rock Candy Mountain

Traditional

Grade 4, Teacher Edition, page 330

●RECORDER 26

Accompanying an Entire Song

After you have sung the song "Johnny Appleseed," compare the song melody with this recorder countermelody. Notice that the last phrase of each piece is the same. Remember to whisper *daah* on each eighth note in order to clearly articulate the rhythm of the last phrase.

From an American Folk Hymn in the Virginia Sacred Musical Repository

Johnny Appleseed

RECORDER

RECORDER 27

Lots of Skips

Practice playing skips between low D and F#, F# and A, and G and B. Remember to say *daah* on each note and to move your fingers together. When you can finger these skips correctly, play the countermelody below to accompany the refrain of *"Somos el barco."*

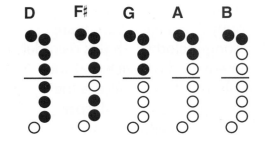

Somos el barco (We Are the Boat)

Words and Music by Lorre Wyatt

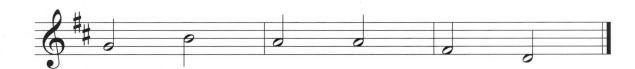

RECORDER 28

Playing Musically

Practice playing the descant below on your recorder. Breathe only at the end of each four-measure phrase. Notice that the first and second phrases have the same melody.

For the Beauty of the Earth

Music by Conrad Kocher

RECORDER

RECORDER 29

Playing with Style

Carefully observe all the repeat markings as you play this countermelody. Remember to tongue notes of the same pitch.

D E G A B C D

Little Shop of Horrors

Music by Alan Menken

To Coda

Two Times

D.C. al Coda

Coda

RECORDER 30

Accelerating Recorder

Feel the steady beat as you practice this
countermelody. When you can play it on your
recorder, play with the recording of this song.
What happens to the tempo during the refrain?

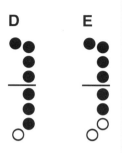

D   E

Dayenu

Jewish Passover Song

VERSE

REFRAIN

RECORDER

I-31

Teacher Notes

ACTIVITY MASTERS

Table of Contents

Name _____   Class _____

ACTIVITY MASTER 1

A Letter to Home

This year, your child will be participating in a music class designed to foster lifelong appreciation of music through active music making. The sequenced music instruction will help your child develop musical skills and understanding, using music of various styles from the United States and around the world. In addition to developing specific musical skills, your child's studies in other areas will be enhanced by instruction that links concepts across the curriculum.

Your child will also have opportunities to participate in theme-based music making. Some possible themes include American music, world music, friends, families, self-esteem, animals, ecology, storytelling, choral singing, seasons, and celebrations. Your child may also be involved in classroom and/or school-wide performances, and you will be invited to attend or volunteer to assist with these performances.

You can also reinforce your child's music learning at home. Consider listening to music together and talking about it. Ask your child to share songs learned in music class. Attend local concerts to help foster appropriate audience behavior. These experiences will help make music meaningful at school, at home, and in the community.

Sincerely,

© PEARSON EDUCATION, INC.

J-2

● ACTIVITY MASTER 2

Una Carta al Hogar

Este año, su niño(a) tomará parte en una clase de música que le ayudará a adquirir una apreciación de música durante toda la vida mediante su participación en actividades musicales. La instrucción de música, que está estructurada en una secuencia lógica, le ayudará a su niño(a) a desarrollar destrezas y conocimientos musicales, al experimentar distintos estilos de música de los Estados Unidos y de todas partes del mundo. Además del desarrollo de destrezas musicales, su niño(a) mejorará en los otros campos de estudio porque la instrucción relaciona conceptos provenientes de todo el plan de estudios.

Su niño(a) también tendrá oportunidades de tomar parte en actividades musicales basadas en un tema. Entre estos temas hay música americana, música mundial, amigos, familias, auto-estima, animales, ecología, cuentos, canto coral, estaciones y celebraciones. Tal vez su niño(a) pueda estar envuelto en actuaciones en la clase y/o para toda la escuela, y se le invitará a usted(es) a asistir o a ayudar con estas actuaciones como voluntario(a). Usted(es) también puede(n) reforzar en casa el aprendizaje de música de su niño(a). Consideren escuchar a música juntos y después hablar sobre lo que oyeron. Pídale a su niño(a) que comparta con usted(es) las canciones que ha aprendido en la clase de música. Llévelo(la) a conciertos de la zona para ayudarle a experimentar en la audiencia conducta apropriada. Todo esto ayudará a hacer que la música sea una experiencia significativa para su niño(a) en la escuela, en casa y en la comunidad.

Sinceramente,

ACTIVITY MASTER 3

Multiple Choice

Select the answer that correctly completes the sentence. Write the letter of the answer in the space provided.

1. The style of singing and the resulting sound is different from culture to culture. Each singing sound has its own

   a) orchestration.   b) timbre.   c) chorus.

2. In Tuva, where one style of singing is based on the overtone series, the people practice

   a) throat singing.   b) opera singing.   c) *mbube* singing.

3. The singing of the Bulgarian women's chorus can best be described as

   a) rough and low.   b) clear and ringing.   c) nasal and pulsing.

4. Classical songs sung by soloists with specially trained voices are called

   a) calypso songs.   b) country-western songs.   c) art songs.

5. The style of singing most likely to have a nasal quality is

   a) country-western.   b) art song.   c) *mbube*.

6. At a Native American powwow, you would most likely hear

   a) only children's voices.   b) men's and women's voices.   c) Bulgarian women's voices.

7. Developed in South Africa, a popular style of male group singing is called

   a) spiritual.   b) throat singing.   c) *mbube*.

● ACTIVITY MASTER 4

Pay Me My Money Down

You can play the harmony part of "Pay Me My Money Down" by using ordinary drinking glasses filled with water. Work with a friend.

<u>What each of you will need</u>
Five drinking glasses about the same size
Water
Paper and tape for labeling
Metal spoon
Food coloring or paint for coloring water
Resonator bells, pitch pipe, piano, or other instrument for tuning

<u>Directions</u>

1. Turn to page 39 in your book.

2. Decide which line of music each of you will play.

   HINT: Your five glasses should be tuned to one of the following pitch sets.
   C♯ D E F♯ G   or   **E F♯ G A B**

3. Put some water in a glass and strike it with a spoon.

4. Try to find out its pitch by comparing it with a pitched instrument.

5. Add or pour out water to change pitch.

   HINT: Because adding water makes the glass vibrate slower, the pitch
           gets lower with more water.

6. Label each glass with its pitch.

7. Add color to the water. It will look attractive and help you remember
   which pitches to play.

ACTIVITY MASTER 5

Creating Rhythms

A. Create some percussion instruments from found materials. Use them as an accompaniment to a speech piece. Describe your instruments here. Tell how you will play them.

1. Example: Keys—shake for a jingling sound.

2. _____

3. _____

4. _____

5. _____

B. Rhythm patterns for an accompaniment: Practice each pattern. Ask friends to join you. Each can play a different pattern.

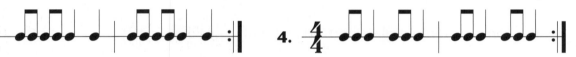

C. Write a speech piece to go with the rhythm patterns. You can change patterns as needed. Try using nonsense syllables along with other words.

Line 1. I can dance the *Macarena*, I can dance a jig.

2. _____

3. _____

4. _____

5. _____

6. _____

If you need more space, continue on the other side of the paper. Plan a performance for the class.

ACTIVITY MASTER 6
Crossword Puzzle 1

adagio	Khachaturian	ostinato	sixteenth	timbre
andante	*koto*	Panorama	*staccato*	tonal
Bartok	*legato*	pentatonic	steel	vibrating
didgeridoo	lute	*piano*	strong	voice
dynamics	Marsalis	*pizzicato*	tempo	weak
forte	McFerrin	*presto*	texture	
interval	measure	*rebab*	tie	

Across
6. When there are four even sounds on a beat, you can write them using ____ notes. (p. 92)
7. Slow (p. 49)
9. The national instrument of Japan (p. 110)
12. A scale of five notes (p. 25)
13. Soft (p. 7)
14. A repeated pattern in music (p. 76)
16. Connects two notes of the same pitch (p. 53)
18. The second beat in a measure (p. 12)
19. The different levels of loudness and softness of sound (p. 6)
20. The layering of sounds to create a thick or thin quality to music (p. 34)
22. When these family members play together, they make a jazz combo (p. 74)
26. An important instrument of the Renaissance period (p. 110)
28. This composer often used the folk music he collected in his travels (p. 73)
29. Fast (p. 49)
30. A smooth and connected style in music (p. 88)
31. An ancestor of the violin (p. 110)

Down
1. A bar line separates one from another (p. 98)
2. An outstanding composer from the Soviet Union (p. 17)
3. Name of an instrument from Australia (p. 36)
4. The distance between an upper and lower pitch (p. 21)
5. The string instrument sound is made by ____ strings (p. 110)
8. Many of his recordings are *a cappella* (p. 80)
10. A pitch that acts as "home" for all the other pitches that happen around it is called a ____ center (p. 26)
11. Loud (p. 7)
12. Plucking the strings (p. 90)
13. The name of a steel band competition in Trinidad (p. 41)
15. A short and detached style in music (p. 88)
17. The first beat in a measure (p. 12)
21. The unique difference in tone color of sounds (p. 30)
23. Walking speed (p. 49)
24. This type of drum is made from oil storage barrels (p. 40)
25. The speed of the beat (p. 48)
27. An instrument with many timbre possibilities (p. 30)

ACTIVITY MASTER 7

Dragon Dance

You can pretend that you are the leader of the Dragon Dance as it moves down the street. Follow the directions below to make a dragon. Then invite some friends to play "*Wu long*," on page 157, as you slither down the street.

What you will need

Colored paper	Hole punch or something to make a hole
Scissors	Four paper fasteners
Markers	A thin stick or dowel 10–12 inches long

Directions
- Cut out the parts of the dragon.
- Decorate the dragon as you like with things like scales, eyes, nose, and toe nails.
- Make a hole at the top of the legs as marked.
- Make four holes in the body as marked.
- Attach the front and back legs with a paper fastener.
- Make two holes in the dragon's body.
- Put the dowel through the holes. Use some tape, if necessary.

You are ready to do the Dragon Dance.

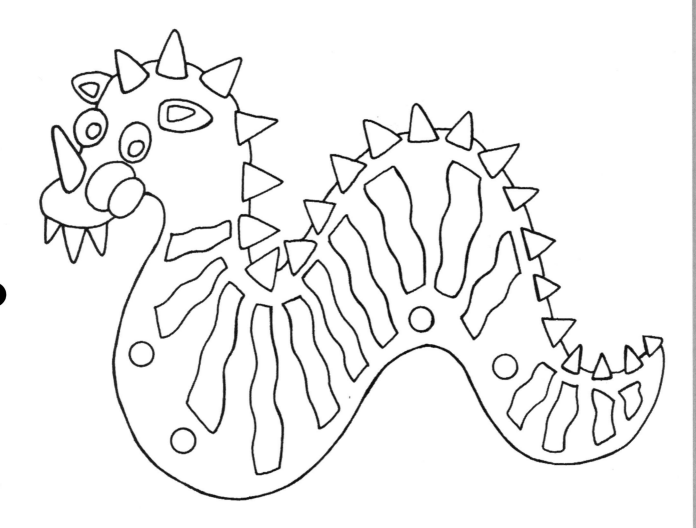

Name _____ Class _____

ACTIVITY MASTER **7** (CONTINUED)

© PEARSON EDUCATION, INC.

Name _____   Class _____

ACTIVITY MASTER 8

Listening

Listen to the recording of "Dry Bones." Answer the questions or follow the directions that are given below.

1. How many sections does this song have? _____

2. Which two sections are harmonized with I and V_7 chords? _____

3. Assume that each of these sections starts on the I chord. Raise your hand every time you hear a chord change.

4. Describe the introduction of the song. _____

_____

5. Are all the voices singing the same part? _____

6. What family of instruments is accompanying the singing? _____

7. Describe what happens to the melody each time a new bone is introduced.

_____

8. Describe the instrumental part each time a new bone is introduced.

_____

9. Are any of the voices singing syllables that are not words?

_____

10. Write down some of the syllables that you hear.

_____

11. Play and I and V_7 chords of Section A on an Autoharp or guitar as the class sings.

ACTIVITIES

● **ACTIVITY MASTER** 9

Find the Question

Here are ten answers to some questions related to what you have learned in Unit 8. Write the question beneath each answer. The answers can be found in your textbook between pages 292 and 319.

1. Answer: Steel drums. Question:

_____

_____

2. Answer: An *erhu,* a *sheng,* and a *pipa.* Question:

_____

_____

3. Answer: Anoushka Shankar. Question:

_____

_____

4. Answer: Diego Rivera. Question:

_____

_____

5. Answer: *La raspa.* Question:

_____

_____

6. Answer: South Africa. Question:

_____

_____

ACTIVITY MASTER 9 (CONTINUED)

7. Answer: James Galway. Question:

_____

_____

8. Answer: Riverdance. Question:

_____

_____

9. Answer: *Balalaika.* Question:

_____

_____

10. Answer: Piotr Tchaikovsky. Question:

_____

_____

● **ACTIVITY MASTER 10**

Tie It Up!

Let's have some fun with ties. The top system has rhythm patterns that you know. Add ties to the eighth notes in the bottom system so that the rhythms match those in the top system. Then say and clap the rhythms. Watch out! The last line is tricky.

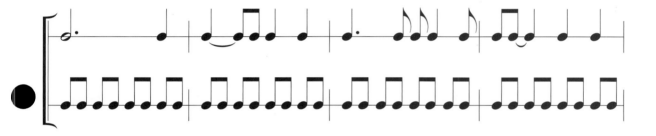

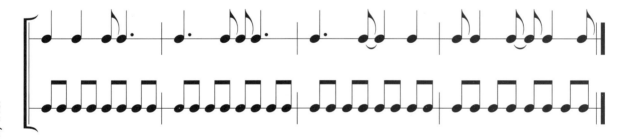

ACTIVITY MASTER 11
Crossword Puzzle 2

Bach	*etude*	ud
balalaika	*gigue*	rondo
Beethoven	glockenspiel	sequence
claves	half	Sousa
countermelody	harmony	*tabla*
Cumberland	key	*tagalog*
Cunas	*Kikuyu*	timpani
Dorothy	maracas	upbeat
ensemble	*ochimbo*	

Across

2. A language of the Philippines (p. 172)
7. A melody pattern that begins on a different pitch each time it is repeated (p. 227)
8. Makes a crisp, rattling sound when shaken (p. 154)
9. A popular dance in the Baroque era of music (p. 232)
10. This composer lost his hearing (p. 153)
12. Judy Garland's role in *Wizard of Oz* (p. 142)
14. One or more notes that occur before the first bar line of a phrase (p. 135)
17. A different melody that is played or sung at the same time as the main melody (p. 159)
18. A type of drum (p. 192)
20. An instrument used in Middle Eastern music (p. 137)
22. This tribe is a farming group in Kenya (p. 135)
23. Native Americans who live on the northern shore of Panama and the San Blas Islands (p. 144)
24. This is the name of the step between the "E" and "F" keys on the piano keyboard (p. 148)

Down

1. This instrument has metal bars that produce a light, ringing sound (p. 154)
2. Kettledrums (p. 155)
3. This signature tells which notes are to be performed flat or sharp throughout a piece of music (p. 148)
4. The _____ Gap is a passage through the mountains of Virginia, Kentucky, and Tennessee (p. 138)
5. This bird is commonly found in Kenya (p. 134)
6. Created when two or more different pitches are sung or played at the same time (p. 162)
11. A practice exercise (p. 157)
13. A musical form (p. 183)
15. A Russian folk instrument (p. 222)
16. In music, a group of musicians who perform together (p. 192)
17. These produce a bright, hollow sound when struck together (p. 155)
19. He composed more than a hundred marches (p. 159)
21. This composer became famous for his ability to improvise on the organ (p. 233)

● ACTIVITY MASTER 12

Going Places U.S.A.

Circle the letters that form the words in the list below.

```
W  E  C  N  E  U  Q  E  S  C  I  D  O  L  E  M  P  N  B  F
W  W  I  P  E  I  R  H  T  U  G  Y  D  O  O  W  W  D  S  G
N  D  A  O  R  L  I  A  R  D  N  U  O  R  G  R  E  D  N  U
A  L  J  O  L  S  O  N  A  M  B  U  T  T  E  I  R  R  A  H
W  C  I  S  U  M  C  I  T  L  E  C  D  U  S  T  B  O  W  L
A  R  E  T  A  E  H  T  L  A  C  I  S  U  M  R  O  U  T  E
C  O  P  S  U  L  E  K  R  U  B  Y  D  N  E  L  G  E  H  T
C  W  I  U  Y  F  L  O  W  A  E  S  E  H  T  E  M  P  O  T
O  W  S  Y  T  A  G  O  S  E  R  B  M  I  T  L  A  C  O  V
M  S  E  G  D  S  S  E  M  T  E  R  C  E  S  B  E  A  T  Z
P  R  E  T  S  O  F  N  E  H  P  E  T  S  T  P  T  J  C  N
A  S  P  E  N  T  A  T  O  N  I  C  S  C  A  L  E  M  Y  I
N  G  C  H  I  P  P  E  W  A  S  I  H  C  A  I  R  A  M  P
I  N  K  J  B  R  Y  A  N  B  U  R  T  O  N  F  K  E  Y  V
M  O  S  X  R  T  M  E  L  O  D  I  C  C  O  N  T  O  U  R
E  S  N  R  E  T  T  A  P  M  H  T  Y  H  R  J  P  T  G  X
N  K  E  A  T  N  A  T  A  L  I  E  C  O  L  E  A  E  M  B
T  L  M  Y  E  N  A  T  K  I  N  G  C  O  L  E  M  V  Y  R
Z  O  F  G  M  J  E  C  N  A  D  R  E  N  T  R  A  P  A  D
Y  F  R  X  G  R  E  S  E  A  S  H  A  N  T  Y  A  Q  W  N
```

sea shanty	musical theater	accompaniment	Woody Guthrie
melodic contour	vocal timbres	route	beat
The Sea Wolf	Harriet Tubman	Natalie Cole	Navajo
Celtic music	Underground Railroad	Al Jolson	Chippewa
rhythm patterns	meter	Nat King Cole	J. Bryan Burton
Stephen Foster	tempo	dustbowl	folk songs
The Glendy Burke	*mariachi*	pentatonic scale	melodic sequence
partner dance			

ACTIVITY MASTER 13

Rondo Form: A B A C A

Create three different body percussion themes. Notate their rhythms here.

1.

2.

3.

Mark each with a letter so that your themes can be performed as a rondo.

Perform your rondo for the class. Enlist some classmates to help you perform your piece.

Add some vocal sounds such as tongue clicks and *shhhhhhh's* to your rondo.

Add some classroom instruments to enhance your new performance.

© PEARSON EDUCATION, INC.

● **ACTIVITY MASTER 14**

Making Instruments

A. Make a list of things that might be recycled in order to create musical instruments.

1. _____   **4.** _____

2. _____   **5.** _____

3. _____

B. Now, consider each item and tell how it could be played or changed to create different timbres. Study the example below.

- egg carton with top slightly open
- egg carton with small items put inside for shaking
- egg carton, cut in half so halves can be clapped together

1. a) _____

   b) _____

2. a) _____

   b) _____

3. a) _____

   b) _____

4. a) _____

   b) _____

5. a) _____

   b) _____

C. Create a short rhythm piece and ask your friends to join you in a performance using "recycled" instruments.

ACTIVITY MASTER 15

Creating New Lyrics

Create new words to "The Twelve Days of Christmas."

"On the first day of _____, *my*

_____ *gave to me ..."*

1st day _____

2nd day _____

3rd day _____

4th day _____

5th day _____

6th day _____

7th day _____

8th day _____

9th day _____

10th day _____

11th day _____

12th day _____

© PEARSON EDUCATION, INC.

ACTIVITIES

● ACTIVITY MASTER 16

Instrument Word Find

Circle the letters that form the words in the list below.

```
W  B  A  G  P  I  P  E  S  Q  Y  S  A  X  O  P  H  O  N  E
B  Q  A  N  A  V  S  F  P  E  W  I  C  C  V  O  J  P  E  F
W  M  E  K  K  S  B  S  T  G  N  C  M  U  O  K  M  C  O  R
Z  V  B  P  I  I  I  J  A  A  O  E  R  D  B  A  U  M  B  E
I  N  X  A  S  A  S  T  P  B  R  C  I  X  R  W  R  A  O  N
Z  H  C  L  E  T  L  M  A  H  G  R  B  A  U  N  D  B  V  C
T  D  T  O  L  O  I  A  U  R  E  N  C  M  D  L  E  M  I  H
E  U  R  I  A  T  R  X  L  G  Y  A  I  A  C  A  R  I  H  H
N  L  U  V  B  U  T  G  D  A  S  O  Z  R  H  R  A  R  U  O
I  C  M  C  M  B  V  I  A  M  B  C  U  R  T  A  N  A  E  R
R  I  P  O  I  A  D  R  U  N  Y  F  O  P  C  S  S  M  L  N
A  M  E  N  T  H  A  R  P  N  J  H  W  R  U  M  B  M  A  B
L  E  T  G  H  T  D  H  A  R  P  S  I  C  H  O  R  D  K  A
C  R  L  A  I  N  Q  G  L  O  C  K  E  N  S  P  I  E  L  S
E  F  Q  U  U  J  T  U  M  E  U  E  N  O  B  M  O  R  T  S
L  O  G  D  T  H  A  K  U  B  A  R  A  D  X  S  Z  I  B  O
L  D  N  H  X  E  E  N  Z  M  X  D  A  T  S  A  R  S  K  O
O  U  V  U  M  H  F  L  U  T  E  J  N  Y  V  W  D  A  G  N
D  N  A  T  I  V  E  A  M  E  R  I  C  A  N  F  L  U  T  E
V  I  O  L  I  N  M  U  R  D  L  E  E  T  S  M  K  O  T  O
```

bagpipes	*didgeridoo*	glockenspiel	marimba	sitar	trombone
balalaika	dulcimer	guitar	Native American	snare drum	trumpet
bassoon	*dundun* drums	harpsichord	flute	steel drum	tuba
cello	*erhu*	*koto*	oboe	string bass	*vihuela*
clarinet	flute	lute	organ	*timbales*	viola
conga	French horn	maracas	saxophone	timpani	violin
darabukah					

ACTIVITY MASTER 17

Keyboard Diagram

● ACTIVITY MASTER 18

Bell Diagram

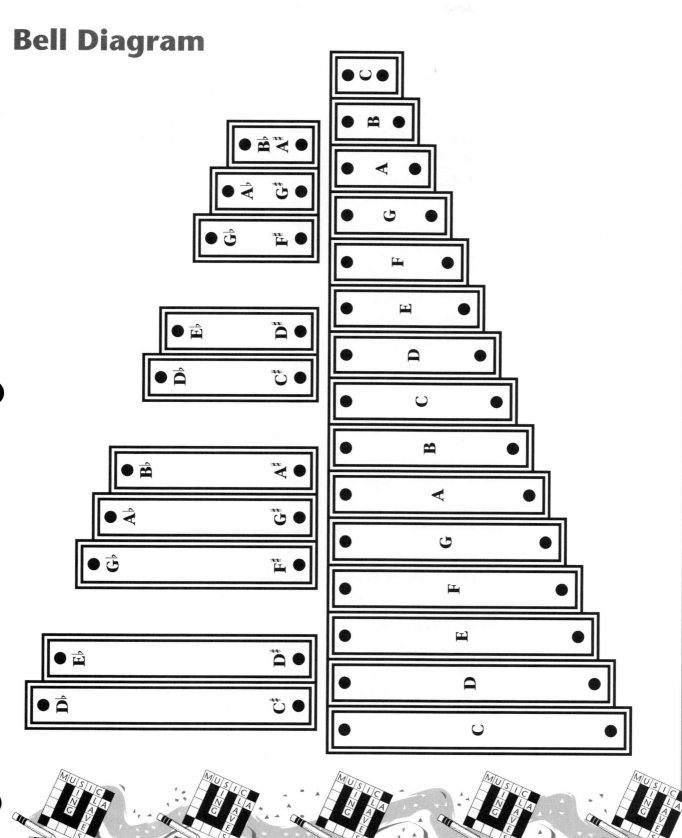

Activity Master 19

Autoharp Diagram

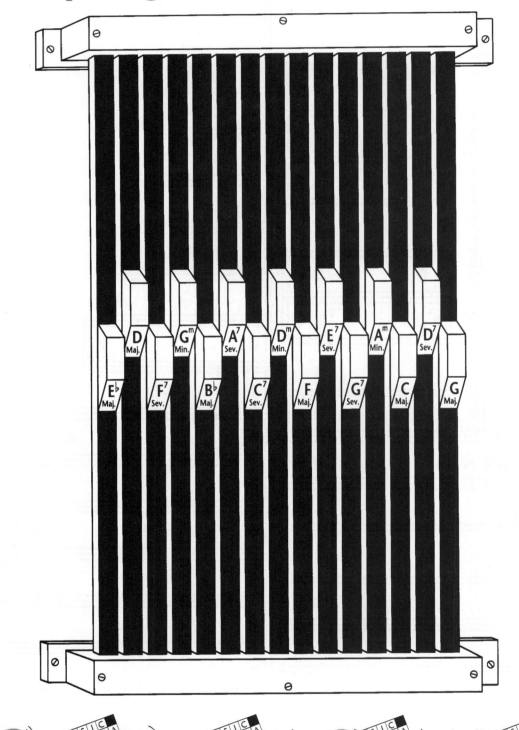

ACTIVITY MASTERS ANSWER KEY

J-4   Activity Master 3: Multiple Choice

1. a) timbre
2. a) throat singing
3. b) clear and ringing
4. c) art songs
5. a) country-western
6. b) men's and women's voices
7. c) *mbube*

J-7   Activity Master 6: Crossword Puzzle 1

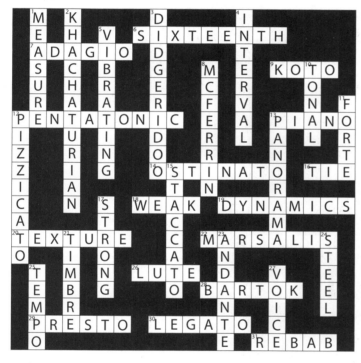

J-10   Activity Master 8: Listening

1. 3 (ABC)
2. 1 and 3 (A and C)

(3.)

4. Voices only
5. No
6. Percussion
7. It moves to a higher pitch (by half step).
8. A different sound effect is used.
9. Yes
10. *Doo, bee, tweet, bop,* and so on

ACTIVITY MASTERS ANSWER KEY (CONTINUED)

J-13 Activity Master 10: Tie It Up!

J-14 Activity Master 11: Crossword Puzzle 2

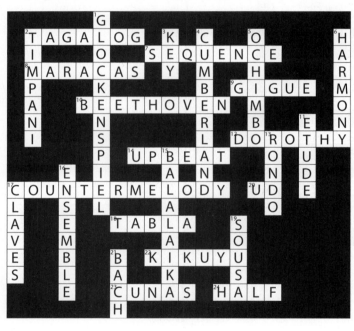

ACTIVITY MASTERS ANSWER KEY (CONTINUED)

J-15 Activity Master 12: Going Places U.S.A.

```
W E C N E U Q E S C I D O L E M P N B F
W W I P E I R H T U G Y D O O W W D S G
N D A O R L I A R D N U O R G R E D N U
A L J O L S O N A M B U T T E I R R A H
W C I S U M C I T L E C D U S T B O W L
A R E T A E H T L A C I S U M R O U T E
C O P S U L E K R U B Y D N E L G E H T
C W I U Y F L O W A E S E H T E M P O T
O W S Y T A G O S E R B M I T L A C O V
M S E G D S S E M T E R C E S B E A T Z
P R E T S O F N E H P E T S T P T J C N
A S P E N T A T O N I C S C A L E M Y I
N G C H I P P E W A S I H C A I R A M P
I N K J B R Y A N B U R T O N F K E Y V
M O S X R T M E L O D I C C O N T O U R
E S N R E T T A P M H T Y H R J P T G X
N K E A T E N A T A L I E C O L E A E M B
T L M Y T N A T K I N G C O L E M V Y R
Z O F G J E C N A D R E N T R A P A D
Y F R X G R E S E A S H A N T Y A Q W N
```

J-19 Activity Master 16: Instrument Word Find

```
W B A G P I P E S Q Y S A X O P H O N E
B Q A N A V S F P E W I C C V O J P E F
W M E K K S B S T G N C M U O K M C O R
Z V B P I I J A A O E R D B A U M A B E
I N X A S A S T P B R C I X R W D E O N
Z H C L S E A T L M A H G R B A U N A C
T D T O I A U R E N C M D L E R A B I H
E U R I V O T R X L G D A S O Z R A M R
N L U V C T U B A T G A V I A M B C U R A N
I C M O N I A H T H A R P N J H W R U M B L
R I P N G R D H A R P S I C H O R D D A K
A M E G C H Q U U J T U M E U E N O B M O R T
L E F T A K U B A R A D X S Z I B S S
C R O G D T H A K U B A R A D X S Z I B S S
E D N H X E E N Z M X D A T S A R S K O
L Q U V U M H F L U T E J N Y V W D A G N
L O G D T H F L U T E J N Y V W D A G
O D N A T I V E A M E R I C A N F L U T E
V I O L I N M U R D L E E T S M K O T O
```

Teacher Notes

● ART CREDITS

Reading
All art Burgandy Beam.

Orff icons
All art Tony Nuccio.

Keyboard
All art Burgandy Beam.

Activity Master
All art Burgandy Beam.

Signing
All art Burgandy Beam.

ACKNOWLEDGMENTS

Credits and appreciation are due publishers and copyright owners for use of the following:

A-2: "Gakavik" (The Partridge) an Armenian Folk Song. Courtesy of Pomegranate Music. www.Pomegranatemusic.com. **A-3:** "Tsuki" (The Moon) from Children's Songs from Japan written by Florence White and Kazuo Akiyama. © 1960 Edward B. Marks Music Company. Copyright renewed. Used by permission. All rights reserved. **A-4:** "Sonando" Words and Music by Peter Terrace. Reprinted by permission of Peter Terrace. **A-5:** "Hashewie" (Going Round) from Roots and Branches. Courtesy World Music Press. **A-6:** "Riqui rán" Folk Song from Latin America, translated by J. Olcutt Sanders. Copyright © 1948 CRS, transferred 1978 World Around Songs, 120 Colberts Creek Rd., Burnsville, NC 28714. Reprinted by permission. **A-8:** "Eh, cumpari!" (Hey, Buddy!) Words and Music by Julius LaRosa and Archie Bleyer. Memory Lane Music Corporation, 1990. Used by permission. **A-9:** "Hey, m'tswala" from The Melody Book by Patricia Hackett, © 1991. Reprinted by permission of Prentice-Hall, Inc., Upper Saddle River, NJ. **A-10:** "Osamu kosamu" (Biting Wind) Japanese Folk Song. Translation © 1993 Gloria J. Kiester. Used by permission. **A-11:** "T'hola t'hola" (Softly, Softly) from African Roots by Jerry Silverman New York: Chelsea House Publishers. **A-14:** "Cantando mentiras" (Singing Tall Tales) from Cantemos en Espanol by The Krones. © 1961 Beatrice and Max Krone, Neil A. Kjos Music Co., Publisher. Used by permission of the publisher. **A-15:** "Ode to Joy" (Come and Sing), Words by Georgette LeNorth. Used by permission of the author. **A-20:** "El rancho grande" (The Big Ranch) Words and music by Silvano Ramos. © 1927 - Edward B. Marks Music Company, Copyright renewed. Used by permission. All Rights Reserved. **A-23:** "Tengo, Tengo, Tengo" (I Have Three Sheep) from the J.D. Robb Collection of Folk Music Recordings at the University of New Mexico Center for Southwest Research. Used by permission. **A-25:** "El Borrego" (The Lamb) from They Came Singing: Songs From California's History, Arlen, Batt, Benson, Kester, 1995, © Calicanto Associates, 6067 Aspinwall Rd, Oakland, CA 94611. Used by permission. **A-27:** "Corrido de Kansas" (Kansas Corrido) from Immigrant Songbook by Jerry Silverman, 1992. Reprinted by permission of Saw Mill Music Corp. **A-28:** "Farewell to the Warriors" from A Cry from the Earth: Music of the North American Indians by John Bierhorst, Ancient City Press, 1992. Used with permission of the author. **A-31:** "Tina singu" Copyright © 1957 CRS, 1976 transferred to World Around Songs, Inc., 20 Colberts Creek Rd., Burnsville, NC 28714. Reprinted by permission. **A-33:** "Bogando a la luz del sol" from Folk Songs of the World edited by Charles Haywood. Copyright © 1966 by Charles Haywood. Reprinted by permission of HarperCollins Publishers Inc. **A-40:** "Einini" (Gaelic Folk Song) arranged by Cyndee Geibler. Used by permission of Colla Voce Music, Inc. **A-41:** "Sambalele" © 2002 Pearson Education, Inc. **A-45:** "La copa de la vida" (The Cup of Life) English lyrics by Robi Rosa and Desmond Child. Spanish lyrics by Luis Gomez Escolar. © 1998, 1999 A Phantom Vox Publishing, Universal-Polygram International Publishing, Inc., Desmophobis and Musica Calaca, S.L. All Rights for A Phantom Vox Publishing administered by Warner-Tamerlane Publishing Corp. All Rights Reserved. Used by Permission. WARNER BROS. PUBLICATIONS U.S. INC., Miami, FL 33014. **A-46:** "Shir L'Shalom" (Hand in Hand–A Song for Peace) Last Song of Yitzchak Rabin. Music and words by Yair Rosenblum, arranged by Michael Isaacson. Used by permission Transcontinental Music Publications. 633 Third Avenue. NY, NY 10017. **A-49:** "Ocho kandelikas" (Eight Little Candles) Words and music by Flory Jagoda from The Flory Jagoda Songbook 1993. Reprinted with permission of the author. **D-6:** "Rock Island Line" New words and new music arrangement by Huddie Ledbetter. Edited with new additional material by Alan Lomax. TRO - © Copyright 1959 (Renewed) Folkways Music Publishers, Inc., New York, New York. Used by permission. **E-3:** "Gakavik" (The Partridge) an Armenian Folk Song. Courtesy of Pomegranate Music. **E-5:** "Tsuki" (The Moon) from Children's Songs from Japan written by Florence White and Kazuo Akiyama. © 1960 Edward B. Marks Music Company. **E-7:** "Rock Island Line" New words and new music arrangement by Huddie Ledbetter. Edited with new additional material by Alan Lomax. TRO - © Copyright 1959 (Renewed) Folkways Music Publishers, Inc., New York, New York. **E-8:** "Hashewie" (Going Round) from Roots and Branches. Courtesy World Music Press. **E-13:** "See the Children Playin'" Words by Reginald Royal © 2000 Reijiro Music, ASCAP. **E-15:** "Cumberland Gap" adapted by Jill Trinka © 1996 Jill Trinka. All Rights Reserved. Used by permission. **E-20:** "Kookaburra Sits In The Old Gum Tree" Words and music by Marion Sinclair. Copyright © 1934 (Renewed) Larrikin Music Pub. Pty. Ltd. All Rights Administered by Music Sales Corporation for the Western Hemisphere. **E-21:** "Missy-La, Massa-La" from Brown Girl in the Ring by Alan Lomax. Copyright © 1997 by Alan Lomax. **F-2:** "Soldier, Soldier" Traditional

Song from England and the United States. ORFF accompaniment © 2002 Pearson Education, Inc. **F-3:** "Somebody's Knockin' at Your Door" African American Spiritual. ORFF accompaniment © 2002 Pearson Education, Inc. **F-4:** "Rock Island Line" New words and new music arrangement by Huddie Ledbetter. TRO - © Copyright 1959 (Renewed) Folkways Music Publishers, Inc., New York, New York. ORFF acompaniment by Pearson Education, Inc. **F-7:** "Paw-Paw Patch" Play-Party Song from the United States. ORFF accompaniment © 2002 Pearson Education, Inc. **F-8:** "Weevily Wheat" Traditional. ORFF accompaniment © 2002 Pearson Education, Inc. **F-9:** "See the Children Playin'" Words by Reginald Royal © 2000 Reijiro Music, ASCAP. ORFF acompaniment by Pearson Education, Inc. **F-10:** "Cancion de Cuna" (Cradle Song) Folk Song from Latin America. ORFF accompaniment © 2002 Pearson Education, Inc. **F-11:** "All Night, All Day" African American Spiritual. ORFF accompaniment © 2002 Pearson Education, Inc. **F-12:** "Kookaburra Sits In The Old Gum Tree" Words and Music by Marion Sinclair. Copyright © 1934 (Renewed) Larrikin Music Pub. Ltd. ORFF accompaniment by Pearson Education, Inc. **F-14:** "Missy-La, Massa-La" from Brown Girl in the Ring by Alan Lomax. Copyright © 1997 by Alan Lomax. Reprinted by permission of Pantheon Books, a division of Random House, Inc. ORFF acompaniment by Pearson Education, Inc. **F-16:** "Dry Bones Come Skipping" Traditional Song from the United States. ORFF accompaniment © 2002 Pearson Education, Inc. **F-17:** "Beriozka" (The Birch Tree) Folk Song from Russia. ORFF accompaniment © 2002 Pearson Education, Inc. **F-18:** "The Bard of Armagh" Folk tune from Ireland. ORFF accompaniment © 2002 Pearson Education, Inc. **F-20:** "Tina singu" Copyright © 1957 CRS, 1976 transferred to World Around Songs, Inc., 20 Colberts Creek Rd., Burnsville, NC 28714. ORFF acompaniment by Pearson Education, Inc. **F-21:** "Sakura" Folk Song from Japan. ORFF accompaniment © 2002 Pearson Education, Inc. **F-22:** "Feng yang hua gu" (Feng Yang Song) Folk song from China. ORFF accompaniment © 2002 Pearson Education, Inc. **F-23:** "Yibane amenu" Round from Israel. ORFF accompaniment © 2002 Pearson Education, Inc. **F-24:** "Wings of a Dove" © Berandol Music Publishers. Reprinted by permission. ORFF acompaniment by Pearson Education, Inc. **F-27:** "Clementine" Folk Song from the United States. ORFF accompaniment © 2002 Pearson Education, Inc. **F-30:** "Cindy" Folk Song from the United States. Arrangement © 2002 Pearson Education, Inc. ORFF accompaniment © 2002 Pearson Education, Inc. **F-32:** "Al quebrar la piñata" (Piñata Song) Christmas Song from Mexico. ORFF accompaniment © 2002 Pearson Education, Inc. **F-34:** "Dayenu" (It Would Have Been Enough) Jewish Passover Song. ORFF accompaniment © 2002 Pearson Education, Inc. **G-2:** "Put a Little Love in Your Heart" by Jimmy Holiday, Randy Myers and Jackie DeShannon. © 1969 (Renewed) EMI Unart Catalog Inc. All Rights Reserved. Used by Permission. WARNER BROS. PUBLICATIONS U.S. INC., Miami, FL 33014. **G-4:** "The Lion Sleeps Tonight," New lyrics and revised music by George David Weiss, Hugo Peretti, and Luigi Creatore. © 1961 Folkways Music Publishers, Inc. © Renewed by George David Weiss, Luigi Creatore, and June Peretti. © Assigned to Abilene Music, Inc. All Rights Reserved. Used by Permission. WARNER BROS. PUBLICATIONS U.S. INC., Miami, FL 33014. **G-13:** "California, Here I Come" Words and music by Al Jolson, B.G. Desylva, and Joseph Meyer. © 1924 (Renewed) Warner Bros. Inc. Rights for Extended Renewal Term in U.S. controlled by Warner Bros. Inc., Stephen Ballentine Music and Meyer-JoRo Music. All Rights Reserved. Used by permission. WARNER BROS. PUBLICATIONS U.S. INC., Miami, FL 33014. **G-19:** "We Shall Overcome" Musical and lyrical adaptation by Zilphia Horton, Frank Hamilton, Guy Carawan and Pete Seeger. Inspired by African American Gospel Singing, members of the Food & Tobacco Workers Union, Charleston, SC and the southern Civil Rights Movement. TRO - © 1960 (Renewed) and 1963 (Renewed) Ludlow Music, Inc., New York, International Copyright Secured. Made in U.S.A. All rights reserved including Public Performance for Profit. Royalties derived from this composition are being contributed to the We Shall Overcome Fund and The Freedom Movement under the Trusteeship of the writers. Used by permission. **G-21:** "Ocho kandelikas" (Eight Little Candles) Words and music by Flory Jagoda from The Flory Jagoda Songbook 1993. Reprinted with permission of the author. **H-6:** "Limbo Like Me" New words and new music adapted by Massie Patterson and Sammy Heyward. (Based on a traditional song) TRO-© 1963 (Renewed) Ludlow Music, Inc., New York, NY. KEYBOARD accompaniment by Pearson Education, Inc. **H-8:** "Joe Turner Blues" Blues Song from the United States. KEYBOARD accompaniment © 2002 Pearson Education, Inc. **H-10:** "Weevily Wheat" Traditional. KEYBOARD accompaniment © 2002 Pearson Education, Inc. **H-11:** "Over My Head" African American Spiritual. KEYBOARD accompaniment © 2002 Pearson Education, Inc. **H-12:** "Ala Da'lona" Arabic Folk Song. KEYBOARD accompaniment © 2002 Pearson Eductation, Inc. **H-14:** "Ode to Joy" (Come and Sing), Words by Georgette LeNorth. KEYBOARD accompaniment by Pearson